# REINVENT YOURSELF

# REINVENT YOURSELF

# A Lesson In Personal Leadership

by John Murphy

VENTURE MANAGEMENT CONSULTANTS, INC.
Grand Rapids, MI 49506
(616) 942-2525

*REINVENT YOURSELF: A LESSON IN PERSONAL LEADERSHIP*

*Copyright © 1996 by John J. Murphy*

*For more information on the concepts presented in this book or to order additional copies, please write Venture Management Consultants, Inc., P.O. Box 6651, Grand Rapids, MI 49516, or call (616) 942-2525, or fax (616) 942-2122.*

*Library of Congress Catalog Card Number: 95-61979*

*ISBN: 0-9639013-2-X*

*Cover design by John Massey, 2131 N. Cleveland, Chicago, IL 60614*

*Pre-print production by Gremel Communications, Inc., 518 Ada Dr., Ada, MI*

*Printed in the United States of America by Eerdmans Printing Co., 231 Jefferson, Grand Rapids, MI*

*Murphy, John J., 1960-*

*Reinvent Yourself: A Lesson In Personal Leadership*

*"...do not worry about your livelihood, what you are to eat or drink or use for clothing.... Look at the birds in the sky. They do not sow or reap...yet your heavenly Father feeds them.... O weak in faith, will He not provide much more for you?"*

*— Matthew 6:26*

A Lesson In Personal Leadership

Reinvent Yourself

# ACKNOWLEDGMENTS

Teamwork is a powerful force. Working together, people can accomplish so much more than they can individually. It may not be easy - trying to reach consensus with multiple points of view - but it is well worth the effort.

This book is the culmination of a true team effort. The advisory and editorial team consisted of Michael Walsh, Ted Gedra, Elizabeth Jennings, Melanie Crispin, Ken Taber, David Murphy, Pete Henderson, Brian Callaghan, Dennis Kellermeier and Dick Murphy. The production team included Meredith Gremel, Lindsey Taylor, Renee James, and Matt Baerwalde. And the cover was designed by John Massey. Thank you all for your honest feedback, insightful comments, and competent advice.

I would also like to thank my parents, Rosemary and Richard Murphy, and my six brothers and sisters - all of whom have enriched my life in profound ways by providing keen insight on the dynamics of human relationships and career choices. You all have such special gifts. Thank you for sharing them with me.

I would also like to acknowledge my wife, Stephanie, and our four inspiring children, Kate, Ben, Kelsey and Jackson. Being a husband and a father is a very special priviledge. Being your husband and your father is a divine honor. Thank you for your patience and understanding as I continue to reinvent myself each and every day in pursuit of becoming the very best that I can be.

# TABLE OF CONTENTS

# INTRODUCTION

**B**efore reading this book, stop and ask yourself this question: If you had all the time and money in the world, what would you be doing?

Now consider a few more questions: What special gifts and unique talents do you have? To what extent are you applying these gifts now to benefit others? Do you consider your work play? Do you look forward to Monday mornings? Does time fly when you are at work? Are you passionate about your career? Are people inspired by your actions and self-confidence? Are you spending your time doing the things that matter most in your life? Are all of the important dimensions of your life - physical, emotional, mental and spiritual - working together? Are you congruent?

Chances are, you bought this book because you sense there is some room for improvement in one or more of these areas. You want a better connection. It's time for a change. Perhaps it's time to start pursuing your purpose in life rather than your paycheck.

This allegory is designed to help you make this change. While the names and characters in the story are fictitious, the relationships and the storyline are based on genuine experiences. By creating an opportunity for you to listen to and observe these characters in action, I hope to empower you with ideas which you can use to turn your own dreams into reality.

As you read the story, take time to make notes to yourself on how you can apply the powerful principles that guide our protagonist, Wayne, on his inspiring journey. Complete each exercise for yourself and look for parallels you can use to guide you on your own journey. While the details of your situation may differ, the principles you will find in Wayne's story are universal and as relevent to your life as they are to his.

# PART I

# Know Your Purpose

"Nothing can resist the human will that will stake even its
existence on its stated purpose."
*Disraeli*

# CHAPTER 1

A loud banging suddenly pierces the still morning air. Squinting my eyes, I discover it is 10:06am. Wow! That tops yesterday. I haven't slept this late in days.

The banging continues. Annette has already left for work, so I have two choices - I either ignore the pest at the door, or find out who it is. I roll over and bury my head under a pillow. It's probably some diehard out selling pots and pans or circulating some petition.

The banging stops. I laugh. The fool has given up.

Minutes later, I spring to my feet. What the hell is going on? Someone's firing up a chainsaw. Annette never said anything about having a tree taken down. I throw on a pair of sweatpants and race for the front door, turning my ankle on my way down the stairs. Now I'm really ticked.

I swing the door open, ready for battle.

Carter Johnston is standing on the step, dressed in a tweed jacket and wearing a paisley tie, throttling a small Stihl chainsaw. Johnston is the outplacement counselor assigned to my case.

"I thought this might get your attention," he laughs.

"What the hell are you doing here?" I yell over the sound of the idling motor. "You make house calls now?"

"You wouldn't return my phone calls. I had to do something to get your attention."

I cross my arms in front of me and stand my ground. "Well,

you've got it. Now what do you plan to do?"

The man flips a switch and the chainsaw sputters to a stop. He then sets the machine down on the ground and stands exactly the way I am standing, with feet apart and arms crossed on his chest.

"I plan to help you," he says without batting an eye.

I feel like punching him right in the face. "Why don't you go waste your time on someone else?" I reply defensively. "I'm doing just fine.

He doesn't budge an inch. He just stares at me, matching and mirroring my every move.

"You call this fine, Wayne?" The man speaks with a confident, yet non-threatening tone. He actually sounds a lot like me.

"Look, Doctor, when I need your help I'll ask for it. Okay?"

"No you won't. That's just it. You do need help, and you won't even return my phone calls."

"I've been busy," I retort.

"I'll bet," he counters. "You've got to work real hard to look like that. Do you have a job?"

What a jerk. I step back to close the door. Johnston steps forward and stops the door with his foot. He's not a small man and it looks like he takes pretty good care of himself. He's obviously not afraid of me.

"Do yourself a favor, Wayne. Go stand in front of a mirror for one minute. Take a good long look at yourself and describe what you see. If you honestly like the man in the mirror, and you look forward to spending the rest of your life with him, I'll leave. Just don't kid yourself. You're smarter than that."

Johnston steps away, and I close the door in his face. He won't leave. The guy's possessed. He's been calling me almost every day now for the past six weeks. Tomorrow he'll probably show up with a bulldozer.

I head for the kitchen. What I really need right now is a cup of coffee, not a look in the mirror. What a horrible thought.

The phone rings. It's probably Annette nagging me to get out of bed.

"Hello," I growl.

"Are you looking in the mirror?"

I don't believe it. Johnston is calling me from the driveway.

"Go away," I demand.

"Not until you're honest with yourself," he replies. "Do as I suggest and you will discover the truth. You need help."

"The truth is, you're a pain in the ass."

"Take the first step, Wayne. Look in the mirror."

I slam the phone down and head for the kitchen. My head is starting to pound from the absence of caffeine, and Johnston isn't making me feel any better. I pour myself a steaming hot mug of coffee and sit down at the kitchen table. The aroma instantly arouses my senses. I pretend to ignore Johnston and distract myself by looking out the kitchen window. A squirrel catches my attention. He sure seems busy, prancing around the yard like he owns the place. What a pest. I fail to realize that this unique little creature is joyfully doing what he is meant to do. He is serving his purpose in life. Then I spot a woodpecker, bashing his head against an old hickory tree. Maybe I don't have it so bad. What could be worse than being a woodpecker?

As I sip my first cup of coffee, I begin thinking about how to spend the day. I could look for a job. It's been nearly two months since I left TYPCO and, sooner or later, I'm going to need the income. Fortunately, the company was decent enough to give me a healthy severance package. That takes some of the pressure off. And with Annette working part-time as a legal secretary, we won't starve for a while. On the other hand, looking for a job just doesn't excite me. Frankly, the thought of going back into plant management turns my stomach. Besides, who wants to hire a 52 year-old?

I continue to sip my coffee and gaze at the woodpecker. Suddenly, he stops and looks at me, cocking his head to one side as if trying to tell me something. Go back to work, I think to myself. Mind your own business! Seconds later, he takes to the air, leaving me staring at my own reflection in the window.

Wow! What a story this picture tells! Perhaps Johnston was right. Maybe I should look in a mirror. I grab my coffee and head for the bathroom, preparing my defense along the way. So I'm a little overweight. Most people are. And maybe I'm not the most attractive person in the world. But I can't change that. I am who I am.

The image in the mirror stares back at me. I lean a little closer. My eyes are bloodshot. My jowls sag like a bassethound's. I have bed-head, and my face is covered with beard stubble. What a sight! Maybe I should be auditioning for a horror picture!

I open my mouth. Instantly, the mirror fogs. Last night's burrito is talking back to me. I gaze deep into my eyes and begin to see the soul of an angry and unhappy man - a guy who has chosen to run from the truth rather than honestly face it.

I step back from the mirror to view more of myself. My paunchy stomach leaves a conspicuous gap between my undershirt and my sweatpants - like something you'd see in a comedy skit. I begin to turn around and suddenly stop. No, I don't need to see the back side. Johnston was right. The truth is staring me right in the face. I am not in control. I do not like the man in the mirror. My external picture reflects an unhappy soul. Somewhere along the way, I've lost respect for myself.

I wonder if he is still here. Johnston is persistent, but not without other responsibilities. I can't possibly be his only client. Or, maybe I am? Maybe he's being punished by his boss? What a sentence - Wayne Peterson, the impossible!

I tiptoe over to the window.

There he is, sitting in his car talking on the phone. Maybe he's getting estimates on heavy artillery. I'll bet he's going to sit there all day. Hah! Maybe I'll let him. Then I realize he's got me blocked in. I'll wait.

During the next hour, I clean myself up and fix a hot breakfast. Johnston is still sitting in the driveway. Evidently, he's got an entire office out there. One minute he's on the phone and the next he's typing something into a laptop. This guy is really possessed!

By noon, I start to lose it. I feel like I've got the CIA surrounding my house and I'm trapped inside. I've got to do something. The man is driving me crazy. Maybe I'll call the police. Nah, that's not my style. A rock through the windshield would be more like it. But I've got to be rational. I know! I'll call him. That way I can keep my distance.

I dial up his office and get his mobile number. Within minutes, the phone is ringing.

"Carter Johnston," the man answers politely.

"Go away!" I say firmly.

"Not until you take a good, honest look at yourself," he replies confidently.

I'm not sure what it is, but there is something about this guy I like. On the surface, he's polished and articulate. But underneath, he's real - no pretense.

"What if I told you I did?"

"Then I'd ask you to describe what you saw."

He's testing me. I pause.

"Well, it's kind of hard to say. I found myself going back and forth between a strong, intelligent, macho kind of guy who belongs in the movies and a frustrated Sumo wrestler who belongs in the circus."

He laughs. "Which one came out on top?"

"I don't know, Johnston. I suppose the jury's still out."

"That's your problem, Peterson." Again he mirrors me. "You don't know who you are."

I walk over and sit down at the kitchen table.

"What is that supposed to mean?"

"It means you've never defined your own direction in life. You've just served as a pawn in someone else's game. You're confused, Peterson. And your confusion is causing you to be bitter. It's amazing you can even see the mirror, let alone yourself."

"How do you know about my life?"

"Because you're obviously angry, and anger is always a second emotion."

He is right about that. I am angry. "But that could mean anything," I argue. "What makes you think my anger is caused by confusion."

"For one thing, I've talked with your former boss, Jack."

"He's also a former friend."

"Anger will do that to people - at least, temporarily."

"That's where you're wrong, Johnston. Jack MacDonald is a permanent former friend."

There is silence on the line.

"That's a choice you make, Wayne, and there is no sense in arguing about that now. In any case, Jack suggested to me that you were bitter long before you lost your job."

"What difference does that make?"

"It makes a world of difference. It suggests that you were never really happy going to work at TYPCO in the first place."

"It was a job."

"No, Wayne. It was the cause of much of your anger. You were a square peg in a round hole. You were not doing what you are meant to do."

This time I pause.

"What are you suggesting - that losing my job was a blessing?"

"That depends on how you decide to look at it. As I see it, you have two choices. You can spend the rest of your life being bitter, or you can turn your life into the most fascinating experience imaginable."

"You've got the wrong guy, Johnston. My life has never been fascinating."

"No wonder you're bitter."

"So what's this got to do with being confused?"

"Call it whatever you want, Wayne, but the bottom line is you don't know what you want to do with your life. You've never defined your own purpose. You've never taken the lead."

"What makes you think I want to lead?" I counter. "Frankly, I'm sick of leading."

He pauses.

"We're talking about two different things, Wayne. You're talking about leading people - as a manager is expected to do. I'm talking about leading yourself."

"You're right, Johnston. We are talking about two different things. And I don't know what you're talking about."

"I'm talking about personal leadership. I'm talking about taking charge of your own life and blazing your own trail. I'm talking about hitching your wagon to a star."

I stand up and look out the front window. Johnston is now sitting on the hood of his car. "And you think this will make me happy?"

"That's right," he answers.

"What makes you so sure?"

He speaks with a firm, yet non-threatening tone. "Living

proof. I've been there. That's the business I'm in."

"Well, I don't believe I have a star. I was always taught to keep my nose to the grindstone and put in a good day's work. Dreaming is for people who don't have anything better to do."

The man is silent for a moment.

"Are you telling me that you don't dream, Wayne."

I hesitate. "Well, no, everyone dreams from time to time."

"Do you listen to your dreams?"

"Look, I don't want to get into this right now. My dreams are personal and, lately, they've been nightmares. Besides, I really don't believe in dreams. I think you're the one who is confused."

"We'll talk about that another day," he suggests. "For now, do yourself another favor."

"What's that?"

"Take time to define your moments of bliss."

"What?"

"Stop and think about the times when you've been most happy and fulfilled. This will help you identify your core purpose in life."

"That shouldn't take long," I grunt.

"Do it, Wayne. I assure you it will make a world of difference."

With that, he hangs up the phone and drives away. What a bizarre morning!

# CHAPTER 2

The day races by. I ignore the advice Carter Johnston gave me and focus instead on building a set of cabinets. I have a wood shop set up in my garage, complete with workbench, table saw, miter saw and a couple dozen other prized possessions. The cabinets I'm working on will go along the east wall of the garage.

I finish priming the cabinet doors and decide to take a break. My wife, Annette, greets me as I walk into the kitchen. She has just arrived home from work and is in the process of putting away some groceries.

"So what did you do with yourself, today?" she asks. Annette never takes long to start a conversation.

"I worked out in the shop."

"You didn't look for a job?"

I ignore the question.

"Oh, that's right," she continues. "You're going to win the lottery."

"Lighten up, Nette." I open the refrigerator and stand in front of it. "I've got plenty of time to find a job."

"You're going to need it, Wayne. Attitudes like yours aren't in very high demand these days."

Sometimes I'm amazed that our marriage has lasted thirty-one years. It seems the last twenty-nine have been nothing but continuous combat. Then again, that's one of the things I like about

Annette. She doesn't back down from anyone, especially me.

"Well, you've managed to do all right," I rebut sarcastically.

Annette smiles. "That's right, I have."

I continue gazing into the refrigerator. "What's for dinner?"

"Maybe I should ask you," she rebuffs. "Seems you're home a lot more than I am these days."

"Nice try," I snarl. "But cooking isn't in my deck of cards."

"Oh yes it is, Wayne," she counters, stepping in front of me to put some milk away. "But for some bizarre reason, you've decided not to play with the full deck."

I start to say something and then stop. This conversation is going nowhere. Annette's been hanging around lawyers too much. She's always got to have the last say.

"I'm going back out to my shop," I huff, turning for the door.

"That's right, Wayne. Go bury yourself. Just run from your problems."

I stop and turn in the doorway. "You think I'm proud to be out of work?" I shout angrily. "You think I'm having fun? You think I like feeling rejected?"

"No, I don't," she replies with her back to me. "But I'm tired of your excuses."

"Excuses? What excuses? You think I'm making up excuses?"

The poised, stoical woman continues putting away the groceries, just as she would if we were on vacation. Nothing seems to shake Annette.

"Don't play victim with me, Wayne. You're not the only one affected by this."

"That's easy for you to say. You don't know what it's like to have twenty years of identity stripped away overnight."

She pauses for a moment and then turns toward me. "That's just an excuse and you know it. Face the truth, Wayne. You're going to be miserable until you decide to change your attitude."

The woman is unbelievable. After three decades together, she can't even muster up a little sympathy. What have I done to deserve this?

"You think it's that simple? You think I just have to change my attitude and, voila, I'm reemployed again?"

"This isn't only about reemployment, Wayne. This is about the quality of your life. This is about your relationships with your family and friends. You've been growing miserable for years and you know it. Now, you're just home more often to whine about it."

That's the same thing Johnston said. My life at TYPCO was a nightmare. Everyday there was some crisis: machines not running properly; shortages of material; customers bitching about poor quality; employees complaining about the dumbest things. And it damn near destroyed my family life, as well. That's what Annette's talking about. She's been pushing me to get out of TYPCO for years.

"So you don't want me around the house? Is that it?"

"Stop feeling sorry for yourself. You know exactly what I mean. You treat everyone around you like they're criminals. You don't trust anyone. It's like the whole world's out to get Wayne Peterson."

"Oh, bullshit!"

Annette turns and walks to within two feet of me. I hold my ground.

"When's the last time you talked with Tom?" she asks. Tom is our oldest son. He works for an advertising agency in New York.

"I don't know," I state firmly. "It's been awhile."

"Try two years, Wayne. That's a long while."

"And I suppose you think that's all my fault?"

Annette steps a little closer. She's now only inches away. "Of course not, Dear. You're the innocent victim. Your son is possessed by Satan. You never stood a chance as his father. Your unconditional love and genuine compassion were just never enough to withstand the powerful forces of evil. You had absolutely nothing to do with it."

Annette turns and swishes away like an opera singer gliding across the stage.

"You know I've tried to make amends with Tom, and he doesn't even return my phone calls."

"I wonder who he learned that from," she says, pouring herself a glass of cranberry juice.

"What is it with you, Nette?" I gripe. "Since I got fired, you treat me like I'm some kind of enemy."

"This has nothing to do with your getting fired. That's simply an outcome. What I'm disgusted with is how you're dealing with that outcome."

I look to the ceiling and throw my arms up in the air. "Well, maybe it's an outcome you're satisfied with, but it sure as hell isn't one I'm proud of."

"That's just the problem, Wayne. Your pride is destroying you."

"My pride has nothing to do with this. I got screwed and that's that!"

The woman stares at me from across the room. "Then it's over for you, Wayne. And you gave up without even trying."

"Thanks for the encouragement," I reply sarcastically. Turning, I slam the kitchen door behind me. "'Til death do us part," I mutter to myself. What a catch!

# CHAPTER 3

The shop is brightly lit with fluorescent tubes hanging strategically from the ceiling. Panels of pegboard line the walls at the far end of the garage, with hammers, screwdrivers, vice grips and a myriad of other tools neatly arranged. Not a tool is out of place. This is the culmination of years of acquisition, hard work and self-discipline.

I moved the shop from my basement to the garage about three years ago. There just wasn't enough room to maneuver anymore. Besides, I like to work at night and Annette was complaining that the power tools were disturbing her sleep. I certainly couldn't argue with that.

I've since insulated the garage, installed heating and plumbing, and even added a private telephone line. As soon as I finish the cabinets I'm working on, I'm going to build myself a desk and credenza for the back corner. The only downside to having my shop in the garage is that the cars no longer have any cover. Maybe I'll build a carport someday.

The shop is a great place for me to relieve stress. It's my fortress of solitude, so to speak. Lately, I've been spending a lot of time out here. I suppose that's because I have a lot of time. Prior to getting fired, I used to come out here at night. Sometimes I'd spend hours just organizing stuff.

I've always loved working with wood. My father never quite

understood that. In fact, we used to fight about it all the time. He used to say, "Wayne, you're too smart for that. Go to school and concentrate on getting a real job. You're never going to be happy working with your hands. Learn to work with your mind." One time, I came home from my high school shop class with a wooden sailboat and it mysteriously disappeared. I think my father threw it away in a fit of rage. After that, I hid all my projects so he wouldn't find them. He thought high school shop was for flunkies and factory workers - people he didn't have much respect for.

My dad was a very opinionated, very conservative, financial guy. He saw everything in black and white, and there was no room for debate. He served as Controller for another division of TYPCO for close to thirty years - right up until the time he died from a heart attack. Personally, I think TYPCO did him in early.

He was also one of the key reasons I joined TYPCO in the first place. He practically insisted that I come to work there. At the time, I was working for a landscaping company. It wasn't the most lucrative job in the world, but at least it was one I enjoyed. It allowed me to be creative and take pride in my work. I had dropped out of college after two years to go into the military. My father went ballistic. After leaving the Army, I hooked up with the guys running the landscaping company. I just didn't have it in me to go back to school.

That's when I met Annette. We hated each other at first. She thought I was an egotistical barbarian, and I thought she was a decendent of Attila the Hun. One day, I was having breakfast in the coffee shop where she worked when she whacked me right across the face. Knocked me clear off my stool! I can't remember exactly what I said to provoke her, but I probably deserved it. Anyway, my friends never let me forget it.

That was the same day I fell in love with her, although I didn't admit it for awhile. She was the only woman to ever really challenge me. She is still the most honest, direct and genuine person I know. I respect that. And to this day, I respect Annette - even though we bicker a lot.

I had to give up the landscaping job. After marrying Annette and starting a family, I needed something more secure. That's when I gave in to my father. He introduced me to a guy named David Stone, who preceded Jack MacDonald as General Manager of the Brockton TYPCO division, just outside Boston. Stone liked me from the start, probably because I was cut from the same cloth. Stone was tough as nails, and nobody was going to pull the wool over his eyes. He hired me on as a production supervisor and served as my mentor until MacDonald arrived six years later.

Jack MacDonald started out as a decent man. In fact, we became pretty good friends. We'd go out to the bar together. We'd often golf or bowl on Sundays. We'd even barbeque at each other's houses on a fairly frequent basis. Annette still talks about him like he's some kind of hero. I'll never forget the time we went to Vegas together for a machine convention. We were up all night taking in the sights and playing the casinos. It's one of the few times I saw MacDonald really let his guard down.

Then all of a sudden he decides he's going to reengineer the division. He says we aren't responsive enough to changing conditions. We need to become more proactive, more agile, more customer-driven. He says we have to organize into teams and delegate more responsibility to the people on the front line. The next thing you know, he's bringing in some high-powered consultant and the whole organization is turning upside down. Before long, I'm being told my job is to serve and empower the people on the line. After twenty-two years in a position of control, I'm suddenly supposed to start teaching people to manage themselves.

So I spoke up. I told MacDonald he was making a big

mistake. I mean, why change something that isn't broken? We were making money. We weren't laying anybody off. We had our heads above water. Why reinvent the wheel?

Three months later, MacDonald's telling me my time is up. I'm in the way. I'm no longer part of the solution. I'm now part of the problem. In retrospect, I should have seen it coming. What a sucker I've been to think he was a friend. What kind of friend would fire you?

Now he's calling me to see how I'm doing - as if that's going to make a difference. Frankly, I couldn't care less if I never speak to the man again. He stabbed me in the back and he knows it. If you ask me, he's just trying to ease his own conscience.

And this Carter Johnston, what a treat he is! I mean, what kind of idiot shows up at a client's house with a chainsaw? And what's this bit about defining my moments of bliss? If he really knew what he was doing, he'd see that I'm not that kind of person. The truth is I haven't been happy in a long, long time. Annette and I do not have what you would call a blissful relationship. We're just like two peas in a pod. And the boys? Where do I even begin? Tom wants nothing to do with me - probably because he blames me for never being around when he was growing up. And Walter? Who knows what Walter wants? He spends nine months a year teaching fourth grade and coaching football. Then he charters boats all summer off Cape Cod. If you ask me, I don't know if Walter will ever get serious about anything.

I walk over and touch the cabinet doors. Good! The primer is dry. They're ready for paint. I grap a can of semi-gloss enamel from my workbench, pop the lid with a screwdriver and begin stirring it with a wooden mixing stick. My mind continues to wander.

Looking back, it seems I was happy right up until about the time I joined TYPCO. That's when I started to feel caged, like a tiger trapped behind bars. Stone was a decent zookeeper, but I was no longer free to trust my own instincts and act on my ideas. It was just "do as you're told" and "don't ask a lot of questions." Before long, I found myself locked in by the security of a decent paycheck and benefit plan.

Over the next ten years, I worked my way up to Plant Manager. Now it was my turn to call the shots. Stone taught me how to take charge of a situation and run a tight ship, and that's exactly what I did. Nothing happened in my plant without my say.

MacDonald was never a big fan of my management style, but he was tolerant - at first. As long as we met our production quotas and the union didn't make too much noise, he would stay out of my hair. He had enough problems just trying to deal with the corporate office.

Of course, my management style had its downside, too. And, unfortunately, Stone never taught me how to deal with that. For example, every time there was a problem, it ended up in my lap. No one dared make a decision for themselves. From 6:00am to 6:00pm, I was buried in details. And then there was the problem of feeling hated and distrusted by half the workforce, just because I had to make some unpopular decisions. Clearly, this was not bliss.

Before long, my relationship with Annette and the boys began deteriorating. I'd come home from the plant like the tiger who was teased and jeered at all day by insensitive observers. My agony was chewing me up inside, and I was losing control.

That's when I started eating - anything and everything. One time, I ate two whole pizzas without even sitting down. The boys talked about it for weeks. Then they signed me up for a hot dog eating contest at the school picnic. I never showed up. Instead, I spent the day at TYPCO trying to get some last minute orders out. The truth is I was embarrassed about myself.

Then there was the shop - my stress free zone. I'd get so obsessed with my projects that even the boys questioned my sanity.

---

When they were younger, we'd spend hours working side-by-side without saying a word. They were amazed at my attention to detail. Unfortunately, they both lost interest by the time they were about nine. Too bad. I had always hoped they might have an interest in working with their old man.

Suddenly, I drop the mixing stick in the paint can and head for the shop telephone. I have to make a call.

# CHAPTER 4

"**H**ello?" a mature voice says into the phone.
"Is this Carter Johnston?" I ask abruptly.

"Yes, it is," the man says.

"Carter, this is Wayne Peterson. You got a few minutes?"

"Sure, Wayne, what's up?"

Carter Johnston is probably in his late thirties. He seems like a decent guy. He's obviously well-educated and confident - almost cocky - but, then, I'd probably squash him if he wasn't. I get the feeling he could be doing anything he wants, but he really likes this career counseling stuff.

"I've been thinking about something you said," I continue. "It has to do with my direction in life."

"Go on," he urges.

"Well, first, let me ask you something." I sit down on a stool in a corner of the garage. "What exactly do you mean by a moment of bliss?"

The man pauses. I sense a smile.

"It's simply a time in your life when you are doing exactly what you want to be doing and you're proud of it. It could be a time when you are working on a project that gives you a great sense of accomplishment. Or, it could be a time when you are helping someone else achieve a goal that will make a positive difference in their life. Or, perhaps, it's a time when one of your dreams is coming true. *You're serving your purpose in life, Wayne, when you are putting your unique and natural talents to work for the benefit of others.* You're doing what you are meant to do - as if you had all the time and money in the world. This often translates into a moment of bliss."

My mind begins racing back over the years searching for clues on my purpose in life. What special gifts do I have to benefit others? How can I help the world? What are my moments of bliss?

Carter continues. "For a doctor, this might involve saving a patient's life or delivering a baby. For an attorney, it could mean putting a criminal behind bars or freeing an innocent victim. For an artist, it might be sculpting a statue or painting a portrait. Not everyone in these roles feels passionate about what they are doing, of course. Some are chasing their paychecks rather than their purpose. However, for those pursuing their purpose, these moments stimulate a great sense of excitement and intensity - what you might call bliss. People often explain that they experience time quickening as a result."

"Time quickening?"

"That's right," the man explains. "It's when you're so focused on what you're doing, that time races by and you don't even realize it."

"But what if you're focused on something you don't like doing?" I ask, thinking of my life at TYPCO. "Couldn't you still experience time quickening?"

"Sure you could, but time quickening does not, by itself, qualify an activity as a moment of bliss. These moments must also give you a great sense of accomplishment - like you have improved the world in some way."

"And how are you supposed to know what your core purpose is?"

"That's the tough part, Wayne. And that's exactly why so

many people are unhappy. They go through life frustrated and confused about what they should be doing. Their intuition is trying to speak to them but they aren't listening to it."

"And you think I'm one of them?"

The man pauses for a few seconds. Finally, he speaks. "What do you think?"

"Well, I'll admit I'm not real happy. It seems like my whole life is being flushed down the toilet. Maybe I am a little confused about what I should be doing." I stand up and start pacing around the garage. "I can say one thing for certain. I don't get very excited about sending out a bunch of resumes and going back to work in plant management. I guess that's one of the reasons I've been avoiding you."

"Then don't," he says firmly.

"Try telling that to my wife," I explain. "And you might want to put on an athletic cup first."

A deep, rich laugh explodes over the phone. "So your wife is pressuring you to go back into plant management?"

"Not exactly plant management," I reply. "In fact, she wanted me to leave TYPCO a long time ago."

"Why is that?" he probes patiently.

"She just didn't like what she saw in me after I started working there. She thought I was out of place."

"Were you?"

"I don't know. I'm beginning to think that maybe I was. It wasn't exactly a giant moment of bliss, if that's what you mean."

"I'm not surprised," Johnston says.

"Why do you say that?"

"It's common. I see it all the time."

"Is that why you've been so persistent?" I ask. "You think you can change that?"

"That's a part of it," the man replies.

"And what's the other part?"

"I love what I'm doing."

I laugh to myself. At least this guy walks his talk.

"So how am I supposed to figure out what my core purpose is? I don't even know where to start."

"Yes you do," Johnston explains. "You've already done that. You start by identifying your moments of bliss."

I walk back over to my stool and sit down.

"Well, that's why I called. I want your opinion on something."

"Go ahead. I'm all ears."

"It has to do with a hobby of mine - woodworking."

"It sounds interesting. Go on."

"That all depends on who you talk to," I say. "This isn't exactly something I've been encouraged to pursue. In fact, it's been more of an outlet for me than anything else."

"And you're wondering if this might have something to do with your core purpose in life?"

"That's right."

"Does woodworking give you a great sense of passion?"

"I'd say so. I definitely get into what I'm doing."

"Does it give you a great sense of accomplishment?"

"Yeah, you could say that. I definitely feel good when I finish a project - especially one for someone else."

"Well, that was my next question. Is it something you enjoy doing for the benefit of others?"

"Absolutely! I love making things for people."

"What about time quickening? Does time fly when you're at work?"

"Definitely! I'm out here until two o'clock in the morning sometimes without even realizing it."

"And you're in your workshop right now?" he laughs.

"That's right," I reply, looking at my watch. It's 7:45pm. So much for dinner.

"Wayne, you're on your way!"

This time, I'm the one who starts laughing. "So you think my core purpose in life is to make things for people out of wood?"

"Try something, Wayne. Tonight when you close your eyes to go to sleep, imagine you can have any five wishes in the world - as long as they are humanly possible. Tomorrow I want to know what your wishes are."

"Anything else?" I ask.

"Yes," the man adds. "Also try to identify your core competencies. You can do this tomorrow by sitting down and identifying several significant accomplishments in your life. Write them down. Then determine the unique talents and skills you demonstrated to achieve these results. These are your core competencies. They are your natural gifts."

"Is that it?"

"No. One more thing. Once you define your core competencies, try writing a short biography on yourself ten years from now. What will you be doing? What will you have accomplished? What will the world be saying about Wayne Peterson?"

"That's a stretch."

"That's right. It is," he says. "But if you want to make a sustainable change in your life, you have to make it in your mind first. You have to see the new Wayne Peterson before you can shed the old one."

"But what about my constraints? I have very limited financial resources. I've got to eat. I've got a wife to think about. I've got a mother-in-law who needs special attention. And I'm 52 years old! How am I supposed deal with that?"

"I understand your doubts, Wayne. We all have constraints

which affect our choices in life. But let's not get hung up on that right now. It will only limit you. Let's begin by defining where you want to go - your Point B, so to speak. This will give you purpose and direction. Once we know this, we can back up to Point A - your current situation, including all of your constraints - and we can begin designing a creative plan to take you from Point A to Point B."

"Sounds like I'm planning a vacation," I mutter in disbelief.

"Let's call it a journey, Wayne. But if we do this right, it just might end up *feeling* like a vacation."

# CHAPTER 5

The house is dark but for one dim light hanging over the kitchen table. Hunched over a stack of papers, I begin reviewing the notes I've made to myself. It's after midnight and my eyes are starting to lose focus. This is so unlike me. I don't know what it is about Carter Johnston, but he definitely has my attention. After talking to him on the phone, I finished painting my cabinet doors. That took me until about ten o'clock. Then I started making notes to myself on some of the questions he gave me. Now I can hardly keep my eyes open. I lay my head down on the the stack of papers for a moment to rest....

---

I awake suddenly to the sound of footsteps.

"What on earth are you doing?" Annette asks, shuffling into the kitchen. "Have you been up all night?"

"I couldn't sleep," I explain, my eyes squinting to focus on the clock. It's 6:30am. "I've got a lot on my mind."

"I'll bet that hurts," she chuckles while pouring us both a cup of coffee. Fortunately, she set the automatic timer on the coffee maker last night.

I ignore the comment.

"So what are you writing?"

"Just some ideas about my future," I mumble. "Nothing to get too excited about."

Annette shuffles over and sits down next to me at the kitchen table. "Mind if I take a look?"

I pull the paper away. "It's nothing really. Just some ideas."

"C'mon, Wayne," she persists. "Try me."

I look into her sincere eyes and slowly slide the paper over to her. Annette knows how to play tough, but deep down, she is a very compassionate woman.

"What's this? Five wishes?" She reads through my list.

---

### MY FIVE LIMITLESS WISHES

1. *To have my family back together again.*
2. *To be financially independent.*
3. *To have my own successful business.*
4. *To be physically fit and energetic.*
5. *To be in command of my own time.*

---

"It's just an exercise I'm doing to try to make some sense out of my life. I learned it from Johnston, that career consultant."

"So this is what you want most in life?" she asks.

"Well, it's a start," I explain. "I have to define what I want if I'm ever going to get it."

Annette smiles. "I like your list."

"Now, I just have to figure out how to turn these dreams into reality. That's what the core competencies and future biography are all about? They're supposed to give me a sense of direction and validity."

Annette skims the rest of the page.

MY CORE COMPETENCIES

1.  *Organization Skills* - good at handling many things at once
2.  *Design Skills* - good at designing products out of wood
3.  *Manufacturing Skills* - good at making things accurately
4.  *Problem-Solving Skills* - good at solving complex problems

MY BIOGRAPHY IN TEN YEARS

*Wayne Peterson is an inspiration to millions of people. Starting in his garage at the age of 52, Peterson built a family dynasty. Joined by his wife and two sons, Peterson has turned a small wood manufacturing business into an international giant. Peterson's story has been featured in many prominent entreprenuerial magazines, and his autobiography is a national best seller. While still serving as Chairman of the Board, Peterson now spends the majority of his time addressing high school students and aspiring entreprenuers on the topic of living your life's dream.*

"Wow!" she says. "Wouldn't that be nice?"

"Johnston encouraged me to stretch."

Annette gets up from the table and grabs the coffee pot. Topping off the mug in front of me, she asks, "So now what?"

"I don't know," I reply. "Johnston's coming back over here this morning to see my shop. He thinks we have a lot of potential."

"He's been here before?"

"Sort of," I explain. "He came by yesterday."

Annette sets the coffee pot back down on the burner. "I wish I could stick around. I'd like to meet the guy."

"You will, Nette. He's kind of hard to get rid of."

# PART II

# Define Your Character

"Things which matter most must never be at the mercy of things which matter least."
*Goethe*

# CHAPTER 6

"So this is your workshop?" Johnston says, poking around in his bluejeans and sweatshirt. The man looks ten years younger when he isn't all dressed up. "Looks like you're pretty organized."

"This is it," I say, gulping down my last sip of coffee. "World headquarters."

"What kind of wood do you typically work with?" he probes, picking up a piece of poplar off my stockpile.

"Most hardwoods, I answer. "It depends on what I'm building."

"Do you use a lot of poplar?" he asks.

I smile. It seems Johnston knows something about wood.

"Fair amount," I continue. "Poplar is one of the softest hardwoods. It's easy to work with, and it holds both paint and stain well."

"I see." Johnston is still making his way slowly around the shop, studying every detail. "What kinds of things do you build?"

"All kinds of stuff. Right now, I'm working on these cabinets. Then, I'm planning to make a desk and credenza for over there." I point to an area in the back corner of the garage. "I've made coffee tables, dressers, nightstands, bookshelves - you name it!"

"Mind showing me some of your work?" he asks.

"Sure. C'mon in the house. There's all kinds of stuff I can show you."

Twenty minutes later, we're back in the shop. Carter has seen my entire collection of things - except for the items I've given away. More importantly, Carter has seen something else - something I didn't realize he was even looking for. He has seen another side of me.

"You love this type of work, don't you, Wayne?" he asks.

"Absolutely!" I reply enthusiastically. "But I never figured I could make a career out of it."

"Well, that's the challenging part. You figured right. You're going to have to do a lot more than you're doing if you want to make a career out of this."

"What do you mean?"

"Let's start with the fact that your dreams go far beyond making a nice piece of furniture." Johnston is referring to my wish list and future biography which he is now holding in his hand. He collected them and reviewed them while we were in the house looking at my work.

"Go on."

"Face it, Wayne. You want to be far more than a craftsman. You want your family back. You want your sons to join you in organizing and building something significant. You want a sense of control over your own destiny. You want fame and fortune. But you will not accomplish these things by simply being a good craftsman. You must become a proactive leader, an inspiring father, and a creative businessman. You must learn to capitalize on your core competencies."

I sit down on my stool. Johnston sits on the corner of a table across from me. He continues.

"And you must also learn to *give*."

"Why do you say that?"

Johnston holds my notes up. "Several reasons. First, look at what you said in your future biography. If you read it carefully, you'll realize that deep down you want to give something back. This is consistent with anyone's real purpose in life. *We are all here to give something.* And the only way we will ever truly realize our dreams is by learning to give that which we wish to receive."

Johnston's right. Deep down, I do want to give people something.

He continues. "Yet, when I look at your five limitless wishes, they offer nothing. They are all aimed at you."

"I suppose you're right. Is that uncommon."

"Not at all," he explains. "But that's exactly why a lot of people never realize their dreams. They think only of themselves."

I sit in silence, wondering if perhaps this is the source of my own ineffectiveness.

Johnston goes on. "Let me ask you something, Wayne. Why aren't your wishes coming true?"

"You mean the items on my list?" I ask.

"That's right. Start with the first one - about having your family back together again."

I sigh. "Well, to begin with, my oldest son won't even speak to me. And my youngest son, Walter - he talks to me but he acts like I'm some kind of alien."

"Do they talk with their mother?"

"Yeah, Annette seems to get along pretty well with both of them. She talks to them or writes to them almost every week."

"So what exactly are you doing to turn this first wish into reality? What are you giving?"

I hesitate for a minute to think about Johnston's question. My first instinct is to defend myself, but I realize that this will not answer his question. What am I doing to bring my family back together again?

"Nothing, I suppose."

"How about your second wish - to become financially

independent? What are you doing to achieve this?"

I think about all the recent mornings when I've overslept. Then I think about all the time I've wasted by not looking for a job. Finally, I think about the hard time I've been giving Johnston - a man who is trying to help me.

"Not much," I reply.

"All right, let's move on to your third wish - to run your own successful business?"

"Nothing," I respond without hesitation.

"And your fourth wish - to be physically fit and energetic?"

"Does this answer your question?" I slap my rotund gut.

"Well, perhaps you're in command of your own time, then?" the man concludes.

"Being unemployed isn't exactly what I had in mind when I wrote that," I say. "I just want to be able to do what I want, when I want, and without worrying about financial constraints and timeclocks and everything else that has controlled my life for the past twenty-five years. I want to be able to say, `Hey, Nette, let's go camping in Vermont for a couple of weeks,' and then do it."

"There's nothing wrong with that."

"But you're right. I'm not doing anything to make these things happen. They're nothing but self-centered pipe dreams."

The man hops off the table. "Then turn them into goals, Wayne. Start making plans. Look for ways to share your gifts with others and get on with it!"

"You make it sound so easy," I say, climbing off my stool. "But I don't even know where to start."

"First, you've got to validate your vision. You've got to make sure this is the direction you really want to go."

"How do I do that?"

"Let's try something," Johnston says. "Close your eyes for a few minutes and imagine that each of your wishes has come true.

Your family is back together again, laughing and spending time together. Your sons look to you with admiration and respect. Annette sees you with passion in her eyes and romance in her heart. Your business is thriving, and your bank accounts are filled with ample dollars. You are in top health - physically, emotionally, mentally and spiritually. You are in command of your own time and living the lifestyle you most wish to live. You look in the mirror and you see a winner. You peer deep into the man's eyes and you see a peaceful soul. You smile and the man smiles back at you, not just because he is happy but because you have freed his spirit and allowed him to achieve his true potential." Johnston pauses for a moment. "Now, come back to the present. Open your eyes and tell me if this means anything to you."

"Of course, it does," I admit. "Who wouldn't want these things?"

"Millions of people," he answers without hesitation. "That's why they don't have them."

"Are you saying that anyone can have these things if they want them?"

"That's right. But they have to *really* want them."

"I don't believe you," I resist. "There's got to be more to it than that."

"Perhaps that's why you've never realized your dreams. You don't think you can."

"I still think it takes more than that," I argue.

"You're probably thinking about the self-discipline necessary to achieve your vision of success. And this is vital to achieving anything meaningful. But what I'm saying is that millions of people - including yourself - have somehow managed to think that their dreams are not even possible. Therefore, they go through life denying themselves the chance to ever achieve them."

Johnston has a point. I have denied myself certain dreams.

Maybe I have elected to view these things as out of reach. After all, I haven't actively pursued any one of my wishes. And I probably wouldn't if this persistent young man were not here rattling my cage.

"So you're saying that I have to first state my desired outcomes and then I have to really want them to make them come true."

"That's step one. And that's exactly where millions of people never even get on the train. They don't define what they want."

"What's step two?" I ask.

"You have to validate your vision," he explains. "You have to make certain that what you want is both meaningful and achievable."

"Is that why we did that little exercise with my eyes closed?"

"That's part of it. The purpose of that exercise is to visualize yourself living your dream. It's intended to evoke specific, passionate, motivating feelings about your future. This sensory vision of success is critical to helping you through the adversity you will undoubtably face on your journey."

"What's the other part?"

"You must also determine if your vision is achievable. Knowing where you want to go is not enough. You must be absolutely convinced in your own mind that you can get there. This is called self-efficacy."

Johnston is right. I haven't really defined what I want. And I certainly haven't convinced myself that it's possible. My dreams are just illusions. I've never turned them into goals.

"So how do I determine if my vision is achievable?"

"Two ways," the man replies. "First, look carefully at what exists now. It is proof of what can be done."

"And the second way?"

"Intuition," he adds. *"Learn to see what others don't."*

# CHAPTER 7

"**W**here are we going?" I ask, climbing into Johnston's mobile office.

"To do some research," the man explains. "It's time to gather some data."

"What kind of data?"

"Facts. Ideas. Options. Reactions." He fires up the automobile and pulls out of the driveway. "Where do you normally shop for supplies?"

"Builders' Paradise," I reply smiling. "It's got everything."

Johnston laughs. "I know the place well."

Ten minutes later, we're walking through the front doors. I have to walk quickly to keep pace with him.

He immediately heads to an area in the store where there is a rack of self-help books for builders. He grabs one and hands it to me. "Start looking for ideas," he says, taking another book off the shelf for himself.

"What exactly am I looking for?" I ask.

"Something you can mass produce out of wood that millions of people want," he says without looking up.

"What about furniture?"

"That's one option, Wayne. We're looking for others."

"Why does it have to be something I can mass produce?" I inquire.

"Because you're going to make thousands of them and that's kind of hard to do all by yourself."

I shake my head. The man is nuts.

"Mind if I go pick up a box of screws?" I ask five minutes later. I'm already bored with this research business.

"Not until we have at least three good ideas," Johnston says without looking up. "We're not leaving until we have three options."

"What about bookshelves?" I ask. "I could make beautiful hardwood bookshelves."

"That's an option," he says. "But you'd be competing with veneer bookshelves that can be mass produced by large furniture companies and priced far below your costs. We have to find a niche."

The man is intense. He's like a kid who is enthralled with a coloring book or a puppet show or something.

"How about some kind of craft - like a picture frame or specialty mirror of some sort?" I ask.

"That could work," he says, jotting a note to himself on a small index card. "Keep thinking."

During the next twenty minutes we skim through nearly every book on the shelf. Johnston has made a few notes to himself but nothing has really jumped at us.

"What about planters?" I suggest. "I can bang out planters in no time."

He writes it down. "It's worth looking into."

After exhausting every resource on the bookshelves, Johnston and I wander aimlessly through the store. The man is noticing things I have never paid any attention to. He stops and picks up an item, studies it from all angles, and then places it back on the shelf. He reminds me of Annette at a clothing shop. She has to evaluate everything, even when she has no intent to buy.

"So what do you think?" I ask curiously.

"I don't know, Wayne. This may take awhile."

---

Five hours later, we return to the shop. Johnston has zig-zagged us all over town. We've browsed our way through at least a half-dozen stores evaluating everything from swing sets to doll houses. Actually, I found the day to be quite invigorating.

"Tell me something, Wayne," he says, sitting down on the corner of a work table. "How do you feel about what we did today?"

I pull up my stool and sit down. "I had fun," I reply. "There sure are a lot of possibilities out there."

"That's right, there are. Now all we have to do is find the one that fits you."

"How do we do that?

"We keep searching. Sooner or later, the answer will appear."

"You don't think we have any answers yet?" I ask.

"We always have answers," he says. "We just don't have the one we're looking for."

"How do you know that?"

He smiles. "Because when we find the right answer, we'll know it. There's no doubt about that."

"So what am I supposed to do now?"

Johnston looks at me carefully. He can sense that I'm skeptical.

"We proceed as if we've found our vehicle. We begin to develop a plan."

"What do you mean by 'our vehicle'?"

"The vehicle I speak of is simply a means of transporting you from your present state to your ideal future state. In your case, it is a product you will sell to the stores we visited today."

"So we were out gathering ideas from my future customers?"

"That's right."

I start laughing. "So I have to identify a product I can mass produce and sell to these big chains?"

"That's one way to achieve your dreams."

"Wow! I never thought about it like that." I hop off my stool and start pacing around the shop. "If I could hook into a big chain like Builders' Paradise, I could sell thousands of products all over the country."

"As long as there is a need for your product," he adds. "You've got to come up with something that people really want - something special."

"And I have to identify a niche," I interrupt. "It's like you said, I can't compete with the big furniture companies. And I'll never achieve my dreams crafting one small piece of furniture at a time. I have to come up with something really unique."

My heart is now pumping rapidly. This is really exciting.

"It appears that you like the idea," Johnston says.

"I sure do," I chuckle. "This is awesome!"

"Well, that validates your core purpose in life and your vision for the future. Now, we have to come up with a plan."

I come back to my stool and sit down.

"How are we supposed to come up with a plan if we don't know the vehicle yet?"

"We take it one step at a time. We know your mission - which is to provide a highly desirable wood product to millions of people - and we know it must be something you can mass produce at a low cost. We also know that you don't have a great deal of capital to invest. And we know that, at present, you are your entire labor force."

"Sounds like we're dreaming," I sigh, losing confidence.

"We are," Johnston explains. "That's all part of the visioning and strategic planning process."

"But are we wasting our time?" I ask. "I mean, doesn't this sound a little unrealistic to you?"

"Not at all, Wayne. In fact, there isn't a doubt in my mind that you can accomplish this in record time if only you convince yourself that you can do it."

"How am I supposed to do that?"

"I'll help you," the young man says. "But first, I want you to do two things. Number one, I want you to read a book titled *Made In America*. It's about how Sam Walton started Wal-Mart."

I think back to the last time I read a book. It's been a while. "I don't read many books."

"You're about to start," Johnston says confidently. "Of course, that's assuming you're serious about making this happen."

"I'll read the book."

"Good. And while you're picking up a copy, make sure you spend a little time browsing for ideas. Maybe you'll come up with something."

"You said you wanted me to do two things. What was the other?"

"Define your character, Wayne. We've identified your mission. But now we need to know what kind of person you're going to become. We need to describe the future Wayne Peterson.

"How am I supposed to do that?" I complain.

"Try these two exercises. First, try writing your own eulogy. What do you want people to say about you in the end? What kind of man will they say you've been? What legacy will you leave behind? What special gift will you bestow upon the world? Second, identify one or two people you really look up to - role models so to speak. Ask yourself, what kind of principles do these people live by? What do they use to guide their behavior?"

"Do these role models have to be alive?"

"Not at all. Many people use role models from over 2000

years ago to guide their behavior. You may choose anyone you please - as long as they give you a clear picture of the kind of person you want to become.

"Why are role models so important?"

Johnston jumps up from the table and extends his hand. I grab it, instantly recognizing the grip of a determined man. It's the first time we've shaken hands. "Because behind every winner, Wayne, there is another winner." He turns and heads for the door. *"Just make sure you choose a winner."*

# CHAPTER 8

The sudden ring of my shop telephone snaps my mind back to the present. I must have been dreaming. I glance at my watch. Wow! It's almost five o'clock! Johnston's been gone for over an hour.

"Hello," I growl, grabbing the phone.

"Did I wake you?" Annette says with a hint of sarcasm in her voice.

"Nice try," I reply. "I've been working all day."

"Hmmm. No wonder you sound so grumpy."

"What do you mean, grumpy?" I growl in self-defense. "I'm in a great mood."

"Oh, that's right, Dear," she teases. "I'm sorry. You always sound like you have your thumb caught in a vice. Have you called 911?"

"You know something, Nette? You ought to apply for a job at one of those 900 hotlines. You really know how to turn a guy on over the phone."

Annette laughs. "Does this mean you'll meet me in the house in thirty minutes?"

I pause. "Are you soliciting business?"

She laughs again. "Not exactly, Testosterone Man. Walter's coming for dinner. I thought I might try to help you with some of the things on your wish list."

Annette's obviously been thinking about that list. I'll bet she sees this as a chance for some kind of reconciliation within the family. I hope she's not too disappointed.

"What time is he coming?" I ask.

"He'll be at the house in an hour. That means you come out of that shop in thirty minutes, not fifty-nine. You've got to stop making Walter feel like he's an interruption."

Annette's probably right. Maybe this is one of those character things Johnston was talking about. I wonder what Walter would have to say at my funeral?

"Maybe I'll come in now," I hear myself say. "How about if I fire up the barbeque? Maybe throw on some pork chops?"

Annette is silent.

"You remember how much Walter likes pork chops, don't you?" I continue. "Why don't you stop on your way home and buy some. I'll get the grill started."

"Why don't you go the store and pick them out yourself?"

There is a pause. A smile crawls across my face. I drop what I'm doing and head for the car.

---

An hour later, Walter steps out onto the back deck where I'm working the grill. Annette and I have had a marvelous time preparing for our youngest son's visit, and I'm in an excellent mood. For the first time in weeks, I feel like I've actually had a productive day. I've taken positive steps in a meaningful direction. Now it's time for me to start taking responsibility for the relationship I have with my children.

"Hey, Walt," I say, extending my hand. "How have you been?"

"Real good, Dad," Walter says, shaking my hand. "How about yourself?"

I turn back to my work and flip a sizzling chop onto its other side. The fires leaps at me.

"I've been great," I lie. The last thing Walter needs to hear right now is a sob story about how his old man got fired and can't find a job. He's heard that before. "I'm keeping real busy."

"Are you getting some good leads on a new job?" he probes.

I flip another pork chop. "Actually, I'm thinking about going into business for myself."

Walter walks around to the other side of the grill to avoid the smoke - or is it to see my face? "That's great!" he says. "What kind of business?"

"Why don't you go get us a couple of cold beers and I'll fill you in?" I reply. "And tell your mom these chops will be ready in about ten minutes."

"Sounds good." He turns and walks into the house. At 25 years old, Walter still looks like he did his senior year in high school. He's a big kid, 6'2", probably 230 pounds, and he loves the game of football. It's just too bad he had it taken away from him so suddenly. Matter of fact, I'll bet he could be playing professionally right now if he hadn't suffered that back injury his freshman year in college. What a tragedy. The kid's dreams were shattered.

Minutes later, Walter is back thrusting an ice cold Budweiser into my hand. "So fill me in, Dad. What's this about starting a company?"

I crack the can of beer open and take a swig. "I'm thinking about turning my shop into a business."

I watch Walt's reaction. He smiles.

"That's fantastic," he says sincerely. "I always figured you belonged in your own business."

"You did?"

He takes a gulp of his beer. "Sure, you just never seemed much like the corporate type to me."

"What makes you say that?"

"I don't know. I guess I see a lot of you in me - and I know I don't belong in the corporate world."

I check the pork chops. They're looking real good. "Is that why you teach?"

Walt takes another swig of his beer. "I teach because I love helping kids improve their lives. Plus, it gives me the chance to coach football."

I pause and look at my son. I just don't understand it. I always assumed Walter was bitter about his football injury. Imagine getting speared in the back by an opposing player and never being able to play the game again. I'd be incensed.

"What about your injury? Doesn't it bother you to be so close to the game without being able to play it?"

Walter looks straight at me - a lot like a linebacker would. "Dad, that happened seven years ago. It's in the past now. Do you think I'm going to live the rest of my life being upset about something I cannot change?"

"But it wasn't your fault!" Aren't you the least bit angry?"

"I chose to play the game, Dad. I assumed the risk. Now, I have to take responsibility for the outcome - as disappointing as it was. Pointing the finger at someone else doesn't change anything. Besides, I've learned a lot by dealing with it."

I shake my head from side to side. "I always thought you were upset about it. I guess it's one of those things we've never really talked about."

"There's a lot of things we've never talked about, Dad."

I flip a chop. "Like what?"

He takes another swig of his beer. "Are you sure you want to get into this right now?"

I look up at my son. "Yes I do, Walt. And it seems you do, too, or you wouldn't have brought it up."

Walter hesitates for a moment. "All right. I'll be straight with you. But hear me out. I'm only saying this to try to improve things."

I flip another chop. The fire hisses. "I'm listening."

He looks directly at me. There is a hint of sadness in his eyes. "The way I see it, we never talk about anything that doesn't revolve around you."

I'm tempted to react defensively but I bite my tongue.

He continues. "For example, you never come to visit me or Tom. You hardly even know what we're doing, not to mention how we're feeling. And whenever we come here, it's always TYPCO this and TYPCO that."

"Well, it's not TYPCO anything anymore," I interject.

"That's not how it sounded the last time we spoke on the phone. You went on for five minutes straight about how the place screwed you."

"You just caught me at a bad time."

"I understand how it feels to lose something you care about, Dad, but you've got to put it behind you. You've got to move on. No one wants to hear it. No one wants to hang around a loser - except other losers."

That sounds a lot like something Johnston said - only I have it backwards. I have to learn to associate with winners. I have to find role models who are proactive and positive. That's obviously what Walter did when he faced adversity. Come to think of it, I don't remember him complaining about it at all. He just picked himself up and moved on. I wonder who his role models are?

"How'd you get through your setback, Walt? I mean, how'd you stay so positive and focused?"

Walter takes a deep breath and looks to the sky. "First, I tried to find the bright side of the situation. I thought about all of the people who had suffered much greater tragedies than I did. Before long, I was actually thankful that I could still walk and run without assistance. My injury could have been so much worse.

I look at my son in silence.

He continues. "Then I started reading about other great athletes who learned to overcome adversity. One of my favorites was Rocky Bleier, a four-time Super Bowl champion who had his foot blown apart in Vietnam soon after being drafted by the Pittsburgh Steelers. The doctors said he'd never play again. Four years later, he was starting at running back with more speed than he ever had at Notre Dame. No one could believe it - except Rocky, of course. He never lost faith.

"So Rocky served as a role model for you?"

"You better believe it! He gave me hope."

"Wow! I never knew that."

"That's my point, Dad. There's a lot you don't know about me."

I pause to think. My son is right. I really don't know what's going on in his life. And I don't have any idea what's going on in his brother's. Maybe I should spend more time focusing on others. "You know, that's what this new business venture is all about. It's my chance to build something for other people. I want to give something back."

Walt drains his beer. "I think that's a great idea! You're a very talented man, Dad. Sharing your gifts with others will no doubt give you a sense of real accomplishment." My son grabs a platter and holds it out for me to load. "So what exactly are you going to build?"

I load the pork chops onto the platter and pull the cover down over the grill. "I'm still thinking about that," I say. *"But I'm going to start by building relationships."*

# CHAPTER 9

"Are you coming to bed?" Annette says, shuffling into the kitchen.

"Not yet," I reply, looking up from the kitchen table. "I have some work to do."

"Want some coffee?"

"No thanks," I say, returning my attention to the paper in front of me. "I won't be up long."

Annette walks over to the table and stands beside me. "What are you doing now?"

"Writing my eulogy," I reply without looking up.

Annette sits down next to me. "Are you planning to die soon?"

I laugh. "No, not that I'm aware of. It's just another one of those visualization exercises Carter Johnston has me doing. I'm supposed to describe myself the way I want to be remembered."

"Sounds interesting." Annette cocks her head to one side and starts craning her neck to see the paper. "Mind if I have a look?"

I quickly turn the paper over and lean back in my chair. "First, let me ask you something. And you have to be perfectly honest, all kidding aside."

"Ooh, that sounds dangerous," she responds playfully.

"You have to describe my character exactly as you see it now."

"Ouch! That might hurt."

"All kidding aside, Nette. I need to know the truth."

Annette sits up straight in her chair and sets her hands in her lap. "Hmmm. Let me see. Wayne Peterson. The lone tough guy. The man who can do no wrong. The man who believes fun is a mortal sin. Want me to continue?"

"I'm listening."

"The man who wants to appear to the outside world as a strong and independent man, but to me is a man who is suffering internally - a once passionate man who has given up hope. Wayne Peterson is a man whose world is now dark, and in his darkness he has lost sight of the most important people in his life. Words to describe the man might include isolated, neutral, insensitive, critical, distant, preoccupied, lonely, aloof..."

"Okay, okay, that's enough."

"...but I still love him." Annette smiles. "You asked for it."

"Well, that blows this eulogy out of the water."

"Let me see." Annette reaches for it.

I pull it away. "You'll think it's ridiculous."

"No I won't. Share it with me."

I slide the paper over to Annette and get up from my chair. "I think I'll go for a walk. I need some exercise."

I stop in the doorway and watch as Annette quickly scans the paper. It reads:

> *Wayne Peterson was a man of integrity. His principles were sound and he walked his talk. If Wayne said he was going to do something, he did it - without complaint. He was a man of wisdom, courage and perseverance. He learned from his mistakes and continued to push forward. He never gave up. He took responsibility for his actions and he always got back up*

*after being knocked down. Wayne Peterson was a
decent and inspiring man. He had a rich sense of humor
and he was kind to the many people he came into
contact with. More than anything else, Wayne learned to
give back...*

"Hold on, Wayne. I'll go with you." Annette grabs a jacket
from the closet and runs after me.

"You want to walk?" I ask.

"Sure, we haven't done this in years. Besides, I could use the
exercise, too."

The night air is cool but refreshing. A full moon lights our
way.

Annette grabs my hand. "Remember when you were in the
landscaping business and we used to go out into the growing fields
and watch the stars?"

"Yeah, I remember."

"Seems like such a long time ago, doesn't it?"

"Sure does."

"Who would have guessed back then that we would be here,
thirty years later, with two grown sons, talking about it?"

I smile. The way Annette puts it, that's more of an
accomplishment than I would have thought.

"It was nice seeing Walter tonight," I say.

"He's a good boy, Wayne. Takes after you."

"He likes the idea of my going into business. Thinks I should
have done it a long time ago."

"I'm not surprised. You two are a lot alike."

"Did he tell you that I'm going to visit him next week?"

"Yes, he did. And he's really excited. You two will have a
great time!"

"He wants me to sit in on one of his classes. He's going to

introduce me as his dad - an entrepreneur!"

"That'll be fun," Annette laughs. "Now, all you have to do is figure out what you do as an entrepreneur."

I grin. "Yeah, I suppose if the kids ask me what I do, I should at least be able to give them an answer."

We walk in silence for a moment.

"Maybe you can tell them you build birdhouses or skateboards or something they can relate to. They'd get a real kick out of that."

I look up to the heavens. What a wonderful thought! Why not build something for children? Or better yet, why not build something that parents and kids can do together? Maybe a ready-to-assemble kit of some sort? That could be my niche! "That's an excellent idea, Nette! I could give people more than just a finished wood product. I could give them an experience the whole family can appreciate!"

Annette smiles and reaches around my waist, giving me a big hug. "Perhaps your visit with Walter will reward you in more ways than you think. Either way, thank you for being such a wonderful dad tonight."

"Yeah, I really had a good time. Walter's an amazing guy."

We walk quietly for a few minutes. A dog howls in the distance.

"By the way, I liked your eulogy." Annette's voice is soft and sincere.

"I have a long way to go, don't I?"

"We all have a long way to go, Wayne. *It's just a lot easier to get there when you know that you're headed in the right direction.*"

# CHAPTER 10

"So this is where you work?" I ask, looking around Carter's office. "That is, when you're not making house calls."

"This is the place," he says. "Let me show you around and introduce you to a few people."

Ten minutes later, we're back in his office sitting at a small conference table. He has introduced me to his entire staff, as well as a few people who have been outplaced like myself. I guess I'm not the only one getting dumped these days.

"Every other Wednesday morning, we have an entrepreneurial roundtable," Carter continues to explain. "You really should sit in on a few sessions. I think you'd find it extremely helpful."

"What kind of stuff do you talk about?"

"Anything and everything that has to do with starting a business - how to write a business plan; how to market your business; how to finance your business; where to go for capital; legal concerns; tax considerations, estate planning. You name it, we cover it! Plus, it's a great opportunity to brainstorm and network with other prospective entrepreneurs."

"Sounds interesting."

"Our next meeting is a week from Wednesday. Can I plan on seeing you there?" The man is looking for a commitment.

I take a deep breath. "Yeah, I'll be there."

Carter leans back in his chair. "So how far into Sam Walton's book are you?"

I smile. I've been waiting for the question. "I read the whole book over the weekend. It's quite a story."

"Well, Sam Walton was quite a man."

"I learned something else over the weekend," I add. "I took your advice and snooped around Wal-Mart a bit."

Carter smiles.

"And I validated a possible product idea. It ties in with something my wife suggested the other night."

"What's that?"

"Well, she thought it might be neat if I made something that kids might appreciate - like birdhouses."

He leans forward. "Go on."

"So I started thinking about it from another perspective - a giving perspective. I want to give people more than just a wood product. I want to give them an experience they can hold on to forever. So I called my son who teaches fourth grade and asked him for his opinion. And he told me that kids love to build birdhouses and feeders. That's when I went to Wal-Mart. And, sure enough, they carry some feeders. But I know I can offer them a better line of products."

"Sounds like you've been listening to your gut, among other things."

"That's right, I have. And I know I can do this. Matter of fact, I'm already building a couple of prototypes to take to my son's class later this week. It's sort of an experiment - research and development, so to speak."

Carter starts laughing. "You know, Wayne, you're a whole different person when you're having fun."

"That's what my wife says."

"Does this mean you've been working on your character

identity, as well?"

"That's right. And I've already come up with two role models."

"Well, that didn't take long. Mind if I ask who they are?"

I lean back in my chair. "The first one is Sam Walton - thanks to you. I knew it as soon as I got into the book. He was a man of courage, conviction, and character. I admire his tenacity and perseverence, and I'm awed by what he accomplished as a businessman."

"He'd be a good one for you to emulate. What about the other one?"

"My second role model is my son, Walter."

Carter leans back in his chair and looks at me. "Now, that one surprises me. I didn't think you two were very close."

"We weren't, but that was my fault. And, this past weekend, I saw some things in my son that I've been overlooking. I found a living example of courage and conviction. I found a man who is doing exactly what he loves to do, and he is not worrying about what his old man or anyone else thinks about it. My son loves his life, and I admire that."

Carter smiles as if he knows exactly what I'm talking about.

"Okay, here's what I want you to do next - in addition to your research and development work. I want you to start studying your role models, and, along with your ideal eulogy, I want you to begin developing a list of guiding principles. These principles, or fundamental truths, are non-negotiable. In other words, they become the one thing in your life that you do not compromise. They serve as your constants. They give you definition and guidance. Working in harmony with these principles elicits honor, trust, integrity and character.

"How many am I supposed to come up with?"

"It doesn't matter. Start by trying to come up with eight or ten. It will be easy once you start identifying the laws by which your role models live."

"What about personality tests and stuff like that? Some people told me that I'm supposed to take a bunch of psychological profiles as part of my outplacement. Is that part of this character stuff?"

Carter smiles. "You can take all the psychological instruments you want, Wayne, if you think that will make a difference."

I lean forward in my chair. "No, I'm not asking for them. I just thought that they were part of the package."

He leans forward and rests his elbows on the table. "Let's take this one step at a time. I may offer you a few assessments later on - depending on circumstances. But for right now, we already know what motivates you and I've got a pretty good indication about your personality type, as well. It's now my job to help you understand these things and capitalize on them. Psychological instruments can be very useful, but there are other ways to discover what you value and need most in life. If you disagree, you let me know. But I trust we're on the right track.

I lean back in my chair. I suppose if this guy can lead me to do some of the stuff I'm already doing, we don't need to get too clinical about what's going on inside my head. What a relief!

# PART III

## Understand Your Competition

"Whether you think you can or you think you can't, you're right."
*Henry Ford*

# CHAPTER 11

I sit silently in the back of the classroom as Walter concludes his morning session. The tiny chair underneath me is absorbing most of my weight but just to be safe, I'm positioned to catch myself should it buckle. The last thing I need right now is twenty-five howling kids witnessing an unexpected, backward somersault.

The class was fantastic! The fourth graders were thrilled with my ready-to-assemble prototypes, and the time raced by as we manufactured three different birdfeeders in teams of five. Every child participated in the process. Some were in charge of assembly. Others were in charge of painting. And then they rotated stations so they all had a chance at each job. Walter and I were the head coaches.

"I haven't had that much fun in a long time," I say to Walter after all the children have left the classroom.

"Kids can be a lot of fun, Dad, if you give them something motivating and productive to do."

"They sure do have a lot of energy," I add. "What I would give for energy like that."

"I don't know, Dad. You seemed pretty energized to me."

Walter is right. My energy level has increased during the past two weeks. I'm getting out of bed earlier. I'm more productive during the day. I've even shed a few pounds as a result of my increased activity and enthusiasm.

"Maybe that's because I'm focusing on something that really motivates me," I say, reflecting on Carter's comments earlier in the week. "I'm not just looking for a job."

"That always worked for me," Walter adds. "Life's a lot more fun when you're doing what you're meant to do."

I laugh to myself. How is it that Walter knows this stuff and I don't? Did I snooze through this class in school? Or do they even teach this stuff in school? I sure don't remember it. All I remember is a bunch of facts and figures.

"So what do you think about the bird products idea, Walt? Do you think I can make a run of it?"

"There's no doubt in my mind, Dad. I think we proved that today." Walter gestures me to follow him out the door. "C'mon. Let's go get some lunch. We've got an hour before our next class."

I follow my son down the school hallway.

"The key, of course, will be understanding your competition and developing strategies to overcome it," he continues.

"That sounds like something a football coach would say."

My son laughs. "The principles are the same, Dad. It doesn't matter if it's winning a game of football, playing in a symphony orchestra or running a successful business. You have to identify and overcome the forces against you. It's the only way to make any real progress."

"What kind of forces do you think I face?"

"Two kinds," the young man says without hesitation. "First, you face *external* forces. You know, like other manufacturers competing with you for business. These are forces you have no direct control over. For example, in football, I have no real control over what the other team chooses to do. All I can do is prepare my own team to deal with it effectively - and, in doing so, possibly discourage our opponents from trying certain things on us. But they can do whatever they want, and we have to be prepared for every possibility."

"And the other kind of competition?" I ask.

"The other kind of competition is *internal*. You know, it's that voice inside you that says you can't do certain things or you shouldn't take the risk. In your case, this voice will apply to your company, as well."

As Walter is saying this, my mind starts drifting back over the past twenty years. My inner voice has been brutal to me. I've been reminded daily about all the things I can't or shouldn't do. And I'm not talking about moral rights and wrongs. I'm talking about career choices and lifestyle and family relationships and my physical appearance and my mental competence. The list is probably endless. No wonder I see an unhappy person in the mirror. I've let my internal competition get the better of me.

We turn a corner and head out into the parking lot.

"What type of competition do you think has more impact on performance - internal or external?" I ask.

"In my opinion, it's internal. No doubt about it." Walter's tone is serious and firm. "I teach the kids that your internal belief system determines your ultimate results in life. If you believe you can, you will. If you believe you can't, you won't. It all starts with what you believe you can and can't do."

"Do you really think it's that simple, Walt. I mean, what if I wanted to become a Hollywood movie star? Do you really think that by just believing it, I could become it?"

Walter stops at the car and looks over the roof at me. "Wanting something, Dad, and truly believing you can do it are two entirely different things. This is where sensory vision and self-discipline come in. First, you have to actually see yourself doing it over and over again. You have to taste it and touch it and smell it and hear it. You have to program your internal belief system to accept it as real."

I shake my head and get into the car. "I don't know, Son. That sounds a little far out to me."

Walter climbs into the driver's seat and starts the engine. "That's exactly why so many people never achieve their dreams. They don't believe they can. And they don't believe in the methods that can reprogram their core beliefs." Walter reaches over and pops the glove compartment open. "Here. Take these cassettes and listen to them. They've helped me immensely."

I sift through the tapes that spill out. Walter's got cassettes on all kinds of subjects - personal leadership, time management, interpersonal effectiveness, conflict resolution. visualization, motivation. Wow! I never realized my son was such a self-help junkie.

"You actually listen to all this stuff?" I ask.

"You better believe it," he says seriously. "I belong to an organization called The Center for Lifelong Learning. The Center's mission is to promote continuous learning for adults. That's where I get the tapes."

"Where do you find the time for all this?"

Walter laughs. "It isn't a question of time. It's a question of priority. We all have the same amount of time in a day. Most people just don't know how to manage it very well. Winners, on the other hand, always find time for their priorities. For me, learning is a priority."

I sigh and think to myself. That's probably where I've been screwing up. I haven't clarified my priorities. I just run from one fire to the next. Maybe I should start by listening to the tape on time management.

I turn and look at my son. "Okay," I say. "I'll listen to the tapes. But I'm still not sure I agree that simply changing your beliefs will change your outcomes."

"Well, don't expect miracles overnight, Dad. And keep one other thing in mind. Your outcomes won't always be positive. It's how you perceive and handle the outcomes that makes the difference. It's how you *respond* to circumstances that determines your ultimate success."

I sit in silence contemplating Walter's words.

"Think of it this way," he continues. "Before you can succeed, you have to learn to deal effectively with adversity. For example, to get a hit in baseball, you have to be willing to strike out. You have to subject yourself to a process that includes both positive and negative outcomes - it's called stepping up to the plate. You can hit the ball, or you can miss the ball. There is risk involved. But you cannot hit the ball if you don't step up to the plate. And people will not step up to the plate if they are not convinced they can hit the ball. It's easier and safer to stay on the sidelines."

"So if I'm absolutely convinced I can run a successful business, and if I'm not afraid to strike out a few times, you're saying I can do it."

"Not exactly. So far, we've only covered the emotional side. Sensory vision and belief stimulate emotion and motivation. This gives you fuel but it does not give you a rational strategy. Studies have shown that the human nervous system is incapable of distinguishing between a physically real experience and a vividly imagined one. Just close your eyes for a moment and imagine yourself biting into a juicy, bitter lemon or watching a thrilling movie on the big screen. If your imagination is vivid enough, your nervous system will react to it as if it is real. This creates a powerful, emotional response. The same thing will happen if you paint a vivid picture of yourself doing whatever it is you dream of doing. It will become even more inspiring if you enhance the picture with color, brightness, sound and movement and you look at it everyday. This is exactly what gets some people to spring out of bed in the morning."

Walter's right about that. My energy level always picks up when I start thinking about my new venture. It's like someone flipped a switch on inside of me.

Walter shifts the car into gear and starts directing us out of the parking lot. "Of course, it doesn't do a whole lot of good to generate a bunch of enthusiasm and motivation without a good strategic plan. You could end up motivating yourself to move in the wrong direction."

"I suppose this is where self-discipline come in."

"There you go. Self-discipline involves setting specific goals and following through with productive action. You want to channel your energy and motivation in a rational direction. Together, your motivation and direction will get you wherever you want to go efficiently and effectively. However, one without the other will do you little good. Just think about all the rah-rah hype that goes on at some of these motivational seminars with no long term effect on people whatsoever."

I nod my head and stare out the window. This has been my problem in the past. I haven't defined my true direction, which means that my motivation - if you can call it that - was coming solely from external sources such as my paycheck and benefit package. I got out of bed in the morning and went to TYPCO because I believed I had to, not because I wanted to. There was no passion or congruency in my life. I was not internally driven.

"Here's a simple example, Dad," Walt continues. "I've got about 3/4 of a tank of gas right now. That means the car's got enough fuel - or motivation - to drive around for about four hours..."

"Are you asking me where we should go to lunch?" I interrupt.

"That would certainly help us make better use of our time and resources." he laughs.

I pause for a moment to think about how much fuel is left in my life's tank. Am I just driving around wasting my resources? Or do I know where I'm going with my life? What is my direction?

"Let's try something healthy," I reply, rejecting my stomach's call for a giant grease fest. "Maybe some place we've never been before."

# CHAPTER 12

As I'm driving back to Brockton from the Cape, I begin reflecting on the past 24 hours with Walter. What a great way to build some understanding and trust in our relationship! For the first time in my life, I feel like I've entered my son's world. I spent the night on his sofa in his apartment. I ate breakfast at his kitchen table - if you can call a couple of file cabinets with a board over them a kitchen table. And I observed my son pursuing his mission in life - to enrich the lives of children.

I also got some great feedback on my birdfeeders. One model was particularly popular, especially with the afternoon classes. At the end of the day, we decided to donate one feeder to every classroom in the school. The principal was delighted.

Walt and I talked for hours. It was different from our past conversations - perhaps because I was on his turf. We talked about dreams and goals and role models and spirituality. Walt shared his philosophy with me that we are not merely physical beings having an occassional spiritual experience. Rather, we are spiritual beings having a physical experience. This really made me stop and think. No wonder it's so important to figure out your mission in life. Failing to do so can destroy your spirit.

We also discussed family and friends and treasured memories. We laughed and joked about old times. Walt even helped me strategize my business plan - an opportunity that he feels brings out the very best in me. Clearly, if my spirit has been suffering, Walt helped me see that it is still very much alive and well. I just have to learn to set it free.

In days past, Walt never wanted to talk much about TYPCO. And we never really talked about what he was doing either. I always assumed he was just goofing off. I didn't realize his purpose and passion in life, and I had no idea he was as gifted as he is. Sure, he was a talented athlete. But when those days ended, he redirected himself to bring new winds into his sails. Now he is extremely well-read, he is an inspiring teacher, he is a winning coach, and he is a soon-to-be published author - a secret he has been keeping from Annette and me until his book is published.

As a teacher and a coach, Walt feels that most kids do not know how to lead effectively. They either don't know their direction in life, or they don't know how to get there. Worse yet, they know what they want but they're overcome by the forces against them. They don't have the self-esteem and the self-discipline to follow through. Walt's book aims at teaching a child how to deal with this. As far as I'm concerned, it's something parents should read, as well.

We also talked about Tom. I explained that I was having trouble reaching Tom and that I wanted to make amends. Walt offered his assistance with one condition - that I seek only to understand his older brother and that I avoid any lecturing or accusation. I agreed and Walt said he would try to set something up. At first, I proposed that we rendezvous at the house, but Walt made it clear that the outing had to be held elsewhere. We settled on either New York or some spot on the Cape.

Perhaps the most insightful part of our discussion was what Walt had to say about competition and character. To be successful, I have to learn how to overcome the forces against me, both internal and external. This includes reprogramming my inner voice and the internal imagery that governs my behavior. He introduced me to a term called NLP, or Neuro-Linguistic Programming. NLP involves using visual, auditory and kinesthetic modalities to change the way I feel about certain things. For example, he showed me how to "dim the lights on" and neutralize unpleasant experiences such as getting fired from TYPCO and replace these negative images with large, bright, colorful, moving pictures of myself in my new role as a successful, energetic entreprenuer. He explained how the human brain has no "off switch" and that if I don't focus it on a positive picture in the future, it will find its own direction - often replaying unpleasant memories from the past over and over again. To change this, he suggested that I go back over any bad or embarrassing situations I've had, only this time I add circus music to it. I tried this and busted up laughing. It definitely changed my perspective.

He also taught me about "dissociating" with myself from time to time by viewing myself from someone else's perspective. This was like looking over my own shoulder - stepping away from myself and asking how I feel about feeling angry or embarrassed or weak or whatever.

The more Walter shared with me, the more I started to relate to some of the things Carter has been telling me. I have to stop and evaluate myself from different perspectives. How do other people see me? What is their perception when I'm arguing or answering the phone or giving directions? Am I likeable? Am I positive? Am I sincere? Am I respectable? Perhaps this all ties in with my identity and character.

He also said I have to learn to associate pleasure with the things I want in my life and pain with the things I don't want. Somehow, I've managed to get the two reversed. For example, I associate pleasure with unhealthy foods and sitting in my easy chair. There's nothing like a deluxe pizza and a bag of nachos in front of the television. On the other hand, I associate pain with things like exercise, risk and admitting mistakes. I've always found it more appealing to take the easy route. To change this, Walter showed me how to associate pleasure with doing things that are positive and appealing. And if they are not appealing to do - like exercise - he taught me to how associate with the positive feelings of having it done.

At this point, I know I've only scratched the surface, but this NLP stuff makes a lot of sense. With Walter's help, I've already neutralized some of my fears and reframed my inner voice to be more helpful and encouraging. Now, my inner voice speaks to me in a more friendly, pleasant tone. Before, it attacked me like a critic.

Most importantly, I've learned something remarkable about my son. He is far more than a school teacher. He is a gift to children. If behavior is organized around beliefs, imagine how successful a child can become by learning early on how to focus in positive, productive directions. I can't wait to read Walter's book! I think his concepts apply as much to adults as they do to children.

Walter also loaned me several cassette tapes to listen to in my car. One of them has to do with principle-centered leadership. Another one has to do with the neuropsychology of success. He even loaned me a few motivational tapes from famous football and basketball coaches. He said the principles apply universally.

As I listen to the tapes, I find myself revisiting many of the things Carter and Walter have shared with me. I also find myself hearing some of the same things Jack MacDonald and Jordan McKay, the consultant, were saying back at TYPCO. I remember Jack stressing the importance of knowing our purpose and defining our character. I think back to some of the exercises Jordan McKay used in the off-site workshop we held. I see myself sitting there in the back of the room, resisting everything he was saying. In this "dissociated" state, I would describe the man in my body as stubborn, ignorant, disrespectful and mean. Wow! Looking at myself through another set of eyes can be painful - and enlightening. No wonder Jack came down so hard on me. He was seeing me as a barrier to growth. I was a tumor in a company determined to be healthy and fit. I had to be removed. It was the only objective, rational thing to do. And here I am shifting blame and responsibility onto everyone else. Maybe it's time for me to associate my departure from TYPCO with pleasure and opportunity - not pain and humiliation. That's obviously what Walter did when he had to give up his football career. He simply reprogrammed himself and moved on.

Suddenly, the voice on the audio program gets my attention. A man is talking about character and principled behavior. He says that attitude is a choice and that sound principles liberate people to pursue their purpose in life with a sense of constancy and honor. Principles give people roots that serve as a foundation for growth and responsibility.

This is what Carter was talking about. Knowing my purpose is not enough. Adolf Hitler had a purpose, but that sure didn't qualify him as having character. If my competition includes the internal forces against me, I would be wise to define the laws by which I will live my life.

The rest of the drive races by. By the time I pull into my driveway, I have twelve guiding principles committed to memory. I quickly scribble them down on a piece of paper.

### MY GUIDING PRINCIPLES

1. *Be positive and proactive - search for the silver linings*
2. *Take responsibility for my own actions and outcomes*
3. *Listen with an open mind - seek to understand*
4. *Be honest, faithful, ethical and forthright - demonstrate integrity*

5. *Cooperate with others - seek win/win solutions*
6. *Be patient and persevere - find alternative paths when faced with obstacles*
7. *Give more than I take - seek to enrich others*
8. *Commit to on-going improvement and lifelong learning*
9. *Commit to excellence - do my very best*
10. *Treat myself and others with dignity and respect*
11. *Have fun - demonstrate a sense of humor and playfulness*
12. *Tolerate honest mistakes - never fear failure*

Circus music starts playing in my mind. I laugh. All the pain and misery I've experienced in the past seems far behind me now. It's over. I may not be able to change what has already happened, but I can learn from it. And I can move forward. My son was right. It's my choice!

# CHAPTER 13

I listen to the message left on the answering machine a second time. Scott Burton? Recruiter? I wonder what he wants. I scribble his phone number down on a piece of scratch paper and sit back in my chair, staring at it.

It always amazes me how these headhunters find people. I remember getting calls at TYPCO tempting me with some mysterious opportunity at the XYZ Company or offering me "the world's most perfect supervisor at a very reasonable salary". Maybe this guy has something in mind for me? Maybe this could save me a lot of headaches?

I stop and think about my guiding principles. I don't see how going to work for another company violates any one of them. It may not be in line with my purpose, but then who really knows if I even have a purpose? If anything, the only principle I'm challenging is the one on being patient and persevering. And is a quick fix really so bad? I think I'll make the call. I might as well keep my options open.

"Mr. Peterson," a friendly voice says. "Thanks for calling me back."

"You're welcome," I reply.

"The reason I called is that I understand you may be looking for employment."

I'm tempted to ask him how he discovered this, but I choose

not to. What difference does it make anyway?

"I might be," I answer.

"You might be? What do you mean by that?"

My tone is serious and direct. "I mean I am looking at all my options and reemployment with another company is only one of them."

"I see," the man says quietly. "Well, from what I understand, you have quite a bit of experience in plant management. You also have a solid track record with a very reputable company. Assuming we market you effectively, I trust we can find you something above and beyond what you were doing at TYPCO."

"Doing or earning?" I interject.

The man laughs. "That's a fair question. I suppose earning is a more appropriate term. My experience is that people often find that they can earn more by moving on to another company. Strange as it may seem, a lot of employers don't recognize and reward their good people well enough. They get all tangled up in these outdated salary systems and point-value formulas that aim at average performance rather than exceptional performance. They forget that the best employees ultimately dictate their own worth in the marketplace. Unfortunately, this often means moving on."

"That certainly was the case at TYPCO," I admit. "We lost a lot of good people to other companies."

"I'm not surprised," the headhunter says.

Suddenly, my mind drifts to the new pay-for-knowledge system that Jack was pushing so hard at TYPCO - right before I left. I remember him saying it was time to start rewarding people for continuous advancement of their knowledge and skills. What a fool I was to resist that.

"So you think I can find another job in plant management earning more money?" I ask.

"No doubt about it," he replies without hesitation. "You've

got a strong background, Mr. Peterson, and you weren't making top dollar. That's for sure. I know. I talked to your former boss."

Why am I not surprised?

The man continues. "The key, of course, is in how you present yourself. That's where I can help. I'm not just a recruiter, I'm a very effective marketing agent."

"I don't doubt that," I say. "But what if I'm not interested in going back into plant management? What if I want to start a business of my own?"

"Why on earth would you want to do that at this stage in life? Let's face it, there's a lot of risk involved in starting a new business. You could lose everything you've worked for."

As he says this, I start thinking about my wife and my sons and my own physical and mental well-being. Somehow, it seems I've already lost what I've been working for.

"Besides," he adds. "You can always start up a new venture after you've retired. Why not pack away some savings for the next ten years and then pursue your business idea? Maybe you can have your cake and eat it, too."

As he says this, my inner voice challenges me to be cautious and objective. I sense this polished stranger doesn't have my best interests in mind. I decide to test him.

"What if going back into plant management isn't consistent with my purpose in life?"

After a brief silence, the man says, "Purpose?"

"That's right," I confirm. "What if I'm not meant to be a plant manager for another company?"

"I'm afraid I don't understand what you mean. You've been in plant management for over twenty years."

"That's right. And it's cost me more than it's worth. Look, I appreciate what you're offering me, Scott. But, somehow, I don't feel like this is the right thing for me to do at this time. I've been held captive by my paycheck for too long. It's time for me to start chasing my passion in life."

"I respect that, Mr. Peterson. But I should also warn you. Thousands of businesses go broke every week in this country. People lose their life savings. Their credit rating goes to hell. Some commit suicide. Others turn to crime out of desperation. Just be careful. Dreams don't always come true."

# CHAPTER 14

Seven people, in addition to Carter Johnston, show up at the entreprenuerial workshop. The ages range from one guy in his mid-thirties to three guys in their mid-fifties. Two women are present, both probably in their early forties. The backgrounds of the group members are varied. One of the women came out of banking. The other was downsized from a large retailer. The young guy was booted from manufacturing, along with me and another guy. There is also an attorney and a designer, both reengineered out of their jobs.

Carter opens the meeting by introducing me to the group. Evidently, I'm the new kid on the block. Following the introductions, everyone gives a quick summary of their entrepreneurial vision along with a short presentation of their business plan. When it comes to my turn, I explain how I'm planning to build ready-to-assemble birdfeeders and birdhouses for the general public. I mention how I have already test-marketed the idea on a class of fourth graders and investigated some of the big retail chains I hope to supply. The more I talk about it, the more enthusiastic I become. Soon, I am standing at the head of the table sketching illustrations of my first three prototypes on a flipchart. By the time I sit down, I have burned up nearly ten minutes on the clock. Then comes my wake up call.

"How are you going to finance the operation?" asks Bill, the attorney. "It sounds to me like you're going to need a lot of capital to get started."

"How will you be able to supply the big chains working alone?" asks Joan, the retailer. "Won't they want to buy in mass quantities?"

"That's a good point," says Joe, the designer. "You're going to have to crank out a lot of product to supply the big chains."

Then the young guy, Michael, jumps in. "And what about packaging? It sounds to me like you're going to have to develop a pretty detailed packaging plan. You know, with assembly instructions and hooks and screws and all that stuff."

I sigh.

Carter just smiles. I keep waiting for him to jump in and offer some encouragement, but he lets the questioning process take its course.

Joan presses on. "How are you going to be able to price this stuff competitively working all by yourself? Won't the big manufacturers have significant economies of scale over you?"

"I don't understand how you're going to market the products without a huge upfront investment," adds Joe. "Advertising alone can cost a bundle."

"You might be better off marketing your products to small niche retailers," adds Joan. "I doubt the big retailers will take you seriously."

A smile crawls slowly across my face. Rather than react defensively like I normally would do, my reprogrammed inner voice advises me to keep an open mind and listen without judgement to what the others are saying. I know I have a good idea and I'm going to stick with it.

All of a sudden, Karen, the banker, reinforces my inner voice. "I think you have a great idea, Wayne. You have a lot of planning to do to pull it off, but that's no different than the rest of us. That's where these workshops can be very useful. Carter encourages us to play the devil's advocate to one another - especially on the first day. It isn't that we disagree with your concept. It's just that entrepreneurial success is often determined by the details. Everyone's got ideas. But it takes some real backbone and perseverence to see them through to fruition."

My inner voice reminds me of a comment Walter made about having a rational strategy, as well as an emotionally compelling vision. It's not enough to have a big idea or to be motivated. I've got to have a good plan. I've got to identify and overcome the forces against me. And these people are not forces against me. They are not trying to hurt me. They're trying to help me. Perhaps I should embrace what the group members are saying as constructive, not destructive. Karen is probably right. I do have to pay attention to the details.

"Maybe I'm getting so caught up in the possibilities that I'm losing sight of a few details," I say. "But your questions are valid and I appreciate that."

My open admission is followed by a brief silence.

Suddenly the room breaks into applause.

Carter speaks first. "Congratulations, Wayne! You've passed your first test. I specifically asked the group to challenge you. If they hurt your feelings, you can blame me."

I smile and shake my head. "I should have expected this from you."

"There's a reason I do this and it's very simple. Every year, thousands of start-up businesses fail because entrepreneurs do not plan carefully enough or they give up too easily. We attempt to eliminate those unpleasant outcomes by attacking some of the root causes early in the process. In other words, I'd rather see you quit right now and find something else to do, as opposed to investing your time, energy and hard earned money in something that will fail."

Joe, the designer, speaks next. "Actually, I think you've got a fantastic idea, Wayne. But Carter's right. I've already gone belly up once myself. And it's because I didn't have a rational plan. I had a great idea, and I had the motivation to go for it, but the details crushed me. I got in way over my head."

"I've had a lot of clients make the same mistake," adds Bill. "In fact, bankruptcy law is one of my specialties. That's why I'm going into business for myself. There's a tremendous need for my skills."

"Maybe we should stay in touch," I chuckle.

"On the contrary," interjects Carter. "You've already got some of the most challenging work finished, Wayne. Finding your purpose and passion in life can be terribly difficult and time consuming. And translating it into a specific vision can be even more troubling. You've already done both. You know what motivates you, and you have a clear picture of where you are going. Now all you have to do is define your competition and develop strategies to overcome it. Your success is just over the wall."

"That sounds like something my son said."

"Good. You've got some wise counsel."

I look around the room. Everyone is listening carefully to Carter.

"Let's hear from some of you," Carter continues. "What forces are preventing you from achieving your vision of success?"

After a short pause, Michael, the young, want-to-be consultant, says, "The biggest force against me is credibility. It's like I said in my business plan, if people don't perceive me as believable, they won't take me seriously, despite what I know. For me, that's a real problem. I'm young. I do not have any advanced degrees. I have not published any books or articles. I have never spoken publicly to a large group. The bottom line is I am not perceived as an authority on anything - even though I know a tremendous amount about Total Quality Management principles and techniques."

And I thought I had it tough. This guy sounds like a real dreamer.

"That's exactly why my plan calls for specific actions to build my credibility. Within three years, I will have my MBA, I will have a book published on TQM, I will be speaking to large groups of people, I will be giving seminars all over the country, and my age will no longer matter."

Wow, I think to myself. Maybe the kid isn't such a dreamer. He sure sounds like he has it figured out."

The next one to speak is Joe. "I've already failed in business once. So I know what happens when your competition gets the better of you. In my case, it happened six years ago when I was trying to go solo as a designer. My greatest competition was my own inability to plan. I just flew by the seat of my pants. I made promises I couldn't keep. I spent money on things I didn't really need. I managed my time poorly. I had no specific goals and priorities governing my activity. I just freelanced myself right out of business."

Why am I not surprised? Joe seems a little wacky to me.

"That's why I've worked so hard on my business plan this time around," he continues. "I've learned a lot about discipline in the past six years working as a corporate designer, and I've learned a lot from this group. I now have financing lined up. I've secured my first major client. I have excellent promotional and marketing materials. I've joined several key groups and associations for independent designers. And I begin teaching a class on graphic design at one of the local colleges next week. That will give me wonderful exposure in the community and broaden my own knowledge base."

Wrong again. This guy is going places.

"My biggest competition is my personality," admits Bill. "There's no doubt about it. It has cost me respect in the past. It has cost me relationships. It has cost me money. In fact, it just cost me my job. I never really paid much attention to people when they pointed the finger my way and accused me of not listening or of being too judgemental or insensitive.

Bill's starting to sound a lot like me.

"I just rationalized my behavior in my own mind and kept right on going," he adds. "This last instance, though, really got my attention. I never expected I'd lose my job because of my attitude."

I can relate to that.

"Anyway, my plan calls for some changes in the way I work with other people. I'm enrolling in some classes on interpersonal effectiveness, I'm reading some great books on the subject, and I'm even starting to listen to some audio tapes while driving in my car. I know the technical side of practicing law. But I have to improve my people skills."

Good for you, I say to myself.

The roundtable dialogue continues. Karen volunteers her poor use of time as her biggest competitor. She explains how she became totally overwhelmed with work by failing to be more proactive and preventive in her management role. People were delegating their problems to her and she became a bottleneck.

"I was spending all of my time managing crises," she says. "I wasn't investing any time in the important things in my life that weren't urgent. For example, I wasn't reading. I wasn't building relationships. I wasn't training and enabling my staff to take on more responsibility. I wasn't developing my own skills and knowledge base. It was like I was on a treadmill. I was busy but I wasn't getting anywhere. Losing my job was probably the best thing that could have happened to me."

What a pity, I think to myself. Or maybe not?

Joan speaks next. She offers her low self-esteem as her biggest competitor. She admits that because she is not really confident about who she is, she has a tendency to exercise her authority in very controlling ways. As a result, she has alienated many of her associates.

"I guess deep down, I'm just looking for a little recognition and appreciation," she explains. "I want people to respect me. And that's where Carter has been so insightful. He's helped me to understand that respect isn't something I can command or dictate - not in the long run. I have to earn it. And in order to earn it, I have to be happy with who I am and what I'm doing. I have to be purposeful and principled. That's now the nucleus of my plan.

As the dialogue continues, I sit silently thinking I have a problem with all of these areas. More importantly, they are all *internal.* Not one member at the table expressed that someone else could do something better than they could. Walter was right. The key force against people is their own internal belief system. Mine has always told me that I can't do certain things, or it's someone else's responsibility or fault. As a result, I've wasted time, I've overlooked resources, and I've neglected people. No wonder I need a plan. Living without one is a disaster.

# CHAPTER 15

At the end of the workshop, Carter asks me to join him in his office. I'm not surprised. The look on my face probably paints a pretty dismal picture.

"That's a lot to take in, isn't it?" he begins.

"You could say that."

"Sit down. Let's talk about it." He gestures to a chair next to his desk. "Tell me how you feel."

I plop into the seat and sigh. "In one word - overwhelmed. Sometimes I just want to go back to my shop and work on my feeders."

Carter leans forward, placing both elbows on his desk. "Be careful, Wayne. That's exactly why a lot of aspiring entrepreneurs fail."

My expression begs him to elaborate.

"Burying yourself in a task is no way to run a successful business. Always remember something - this is a business, not a craft. To grow a successful business, you've got to learn to spend more time working *on* the business system, not *in* the business system. Many people going into business for themselves fail to make this distinction. They like doing a certain task so they try to make a business out of it. Unfortunately, they end up spending most of their time working on the task, not on the business."

"That sounds like what I've been doing."

"It could be if you're not careful. That's why I'm suggesting you think this through a little more deliberately. You've got to engineer a business system that works, not just a birdhouse that works."

He's got a point. When things get tough, I tend to bury myself in my craft. I don't think about reengineering the system that got me into the problem. Instead, I just put my head down and try to weather the storm. That's probably why so many of my problems keep coming back.

"How am I supposed to find time to work on the system when I don't have anyone to work in the system?"

"That's a good question. In fact, now that you've asked it, you're more likely to find an answer."

"What do you mean by that?"

Carter leans back in his chair. "By that, I mean many entrepreneurs would never even think to ask it. And if you never ask the question, you'll never find the answer. Remember the old Biblical phase, seek and ye shall find?"

"Is that another way of saying you aren't going to tell me the answer?"

The man laughs. "No, that's another way of telling you I don't know the answer. All I can tell you is that there are many creative ways to accomplish your goals. In this case, you could explore hiring or subcontracting help, outsourcing work, or getting friends to assist you with things you can't handle yourself. In any case, you are responsible for setting up a system that works effectively and efficiently. And it will be this system, not your individual work effort, that makes or breaks your business."

Wow! I never thought of it that way. From what Carter is saying, I could work my tail off and still fail if the system I'm working in isn't effective. And here I am thinking I can just crank out birdhouses to the giant retailers of the world. Who am I kidding?

"Well, like I said, this whole thing sounds nice, but I'm afraid it's a little overwhelming for me. Maybe I should just go back into plant management. Did I tell you that a recruiter has been calling me? He says I could be making a lot more money with a lot less risk by going back into plant management."

Carter smiles. "Do you believe that's the right thing to do?"

"I don't know what to believe right now. My brain tells me to play it safe and take what I can get. But my gut tells me to follow my dreams. It's like I'm torn up inside. I don't know what to do. And then there's all these details to take care of just to get my business off the ground."

"I'll bet you're used to having other people take care of most of the details. Am I right?"

"That's fair."

"And right now, you see this huge pile of work staring you in the face and you have no one to help you."

I say nothing.

"So you're tempted to give up. You believe it's going to be easier filling a link in someone else's chain rather than building a chain of your own. Right?"

"Well, maybe," I challenge. "Is that so bad?"

"That depends upon the person," Carter replies. "And, in your case, it isn't where your heart is. That means you'll never be truly committed. You'll never be passionate about your work. You'll simply fill up your time and cover your expenses and hope to someday be free again. But your dreams will always remain out of reach because you'll only think about them - you'll never actually go after them."

"Sounds like another TYPCO," I mutter.

"Could be even worse," the man explains. "This time you'll carry the weight of regret with you."

"What do you mean by that?"

"You'll wake up every morning wondering 'What if I had pursued my dreams? What if I had taken the chance?' You may even feel like you just let the opportunity of a lifetime slip through your fingertips." Carter rocks back in his chair and folds his hands in front of him. "Remember something, Wayne. *The weight of discipline is nothing compared to the weight of regret.*"

"So you're saying I shouldn't give up."

"That's your decision, and I'll help you either way. But think carefully about this, Wayne. You have a lot more resources available to you than you think. You just have to learn how to identify them and get them working for you."

"Like what?"

"You name it! Tax. Accounting. Insurance. Marketing. Legal work. Administrative work. Production. Packaging. Shipping. Printing. Design. Selling. Whatever you need."

Carter's right. These days there are all kinds of services available.

"Not to mention books, audios, videos, seminars, classes," he continues. "You can find whatever you want. You just have to know what you're looking for."

"That reminds me," I interject. "Have you ever heard of NLP?"

"Sure I have," the man smiles. "It's very powerful. Where did you learn about NLP?"

"My son Walter explained it to me. In fact, he gave me a cassette on it to listen to."

"Go on."

"Well, I'm impressed with it. I'm already thinking differently about certain things. For example, when I was getting blasted by everybody in the roundtable group, I could hear my inner voice advising me to respond openly and without judgement. Normally, I would have put up a big fight. And when this recruiter called, I could hear my inner voice challenging me to think at a deeper level."

"That's progress."

"And I'm beginning to see my separation from TYPCO as a bright and positive opportunity, not a dark and humiliating failure."

"That's definite progress! How you choose to respond to any given situation will unquestionably affect your ultimate outcomes in life. Some people call it 'managing the gap' between stimulus and response. *We always have a choice in how we respond.* NLP can be very helpful here.

"Well, that's where this gets a little overwhelming," I confess. "I realize I have to move forward rationally and responsibly, but I'm not even sure where to start. I mean, building a business is no small task. I don't think NLP is going to teach me how to set up a business."

Carter reaches into a desk drawer and pulls out a typed document. He then slides it across the desk to me. "That's why I've prepared this list of questions for you. Use it as a checklist. Nearly everything you need to consider in getting started is covered by one of these questions."

I peruse the list. It's broken down into four major parts - Management, Marketing, Operations and Finance - and it's loaded with questions.

## MANAGEMENT

1. Who is organizing this business?
2. What are the entrepreneur's credentials and core competencies?
3. What is the reason for starting this business?
4. What is the purpose or mission of this business?

5. What are the values and guiding principles of this business?
6. What type of business will this be (e.g. S-corporation)? Why?
7. What are the business's critical success factors?
8. What specific factors could destroy this business?
9. What outside assistance will be involved in running the business?
10. Who are the officers of the new company?
11. Will there be a board of directors? If so, who will serve?
12. What is the organizational structure of the company?
13. Describe the decision making process for the new company.
14. Describe the role of Management.
15. How will Management measure its own effectiveness?
16. What specific tasks will be necessary to run the business?
17. Who will complete these tasks?
18. How many employees are forecasted for the next three years?
19. How will you staff the company?
20. What criteria will you used in selecting employees?
21. How will you compensate and reward your employees?
22. Describe any additional benefits to be offered to employees.
23. Will employees be under any type of contract? If so, describe.
24. What kind of training will you offer?
25. Describe all initial employment policies and procedures.
26. Describe all required insurances and provisions for employees.

# MARKETING

1. What will you name this business? Why?
2. How will you identify this business (e.g. logo, slogan,...)?
3. What will the company letterhead look like?
4. What about cards, stationery, envelopes, brochures, labels, etc.?
5. How will you become recognized in the marketplace?
6. How will you sell the products?
7. Who will sell the products?
8. How many sales people will you need?
9. How many different products will you offer? What are they?
10. Who else offers these products?
11. What advantages do you have over your competition?
12. What advantages does your competition have over you?
13. How will you price your products? How does this compare?
14. How will you distribute your products?
15. Who will you target as your primary customers? Why?
16. How big of a geographic area will you market to?
17. What are your primary marketing objectives?
18. What is your marketing budget? How will this money be allocated?
19. Why are your products needed or desired? How do you know?
20. What are your sales projections for the next three years?
21. What methods will you use to stimulate demand for your products?
22. What new products will you offer in the future?
23. Who will be responsible for developing new products?

24. What systems will be necessary to market and sell your products?
25. How will you solicit customer feedback? What will you measure?

## OPERATIONS

1. Define your operating strategy.
2. How is this better than your outside competitors'?
3. Describe your methods of operation.
4. How will these methods be carried out consistently?
5. What standards will be set to assure optimal quality?
6. What standards will be set to assure optimal productivity?
7. What training will be needed to accomplish operational goals?
8. How will this training be provided? Who will provide it?
9. Describe all operational policies and procedures.
10. Describe all safety policies and procedures.
11. What materials will be necessary to run this business?
12. Where will these materials come from?
13. How will suppliers be selected and managed?
14. How will incoming materials be evaluated for quality?
15. How will inventory be managed?
16. What equipment will be necessary to run this business?
17. Where will this equipment come from and under what terms?
18. Describe your forecasted monthly throughput (i.e. quantity).
19. Describe the location(s) of this business.
20. What are the company's expansion plans?
21. Describe all measurement systems (quality, safety, throughput,..)

22. How will information be stored within the company?
23. What information systems will be used?
24. How will security be handled?
25. Describe all required insurance coverages for operations.

## FINANCE

1. What are the company's start-up costs?
2. Describe the initial capital structure for the business?
3. How will funding be raised?
4. Describe the incentives for investors.
5. How will funding be allocated?
6. Define the budget.
7. How are costs determined and how will they be controlled?
8. How will the company's financial results be reported? To whom?
9. How will internal auditing take place? How often? By whom?
10. How will external auditing and tax matters be handled? By whom?
11. What are your financial projections for the next three years?
    a. Income Statement  e. Working Capital
    b. Balance Sheet      d. Breakeven Points
    c. Cash Flow          f. Sources and Uses of Funds
12. How will cash be managed?
13. What accounting method will be used? Why this method?
14. What accounting procedures will be used?
15. How will fixed assets be depreciated?
16. How will payroll be handled? Taxes? Reporting?
17. Will you handle your own receivables? If so, what will

your standard terms be?

18. Who will be responsible for overseeing Accounting and Finance?
19. How will profit be allocated?
20. What strategies will be used to minimize taxes?
21. What kind of returns are forecasted for investors?
22. Identify all financial risks for investors.
23. What will happen in the event of the business leader's death?
24. Describe all personal insurance coverages on the business leader.

"Well, this certainly gives me plenty to think about," I sigh.

"It's not as overwhelming as it looks, Wayne. Believe me. Just try breaking it down into manageable projects and you might be surprised by how quickly you make progress."

I look the list over again. "Got any suggestions on where to start?"

The man leans forward. "You already have the answers to a lot of these questions. You just haven't written them down yet. Try starting with your critical success factors. In other words, list all of the things you need in order to succeed. This will tell you whether or not to continue."

"Are you saying my business plan might talk me out of my venture?"

"Yes, I am. In fact, that's one of the most important reasons to write one."

I smile. "I guess I never thought of it that way."

Carter returns a smile. "Perhaps it's time to think differently."

# PART IV

## Challenge Your Assumptions

"The significant problems we face cannot be solved at the same
level of thinking we were at when we created them."

*Albert Einstein*

# CHAPTER 16

"What are you doing now?" Annette asks, waltzing into the kitchen.

"Working on my business plan," I reply. Until my new desk is built, the kitchen table has become my temporary corporate headquarters.

She glides over to the table. "How's it coming?"

I lean back in my chair and sigh. "It's a pain in the ass. There's so much detail to consider. I'm beginning to wonder if it's all worth it."

"Well, judging from your more recent behavior, I'd say it's well worth it." Annette is speaking about some of the changes I've made in my personal life during the past few weeks. I'm getting up earlier. I'm nicer. I'm more focused. I'm eating healthier foods. I'm drinking twelve glasses of water everyday. I'm going for a walk every night. Who knows? Maybe I'll start bicycling or jogging soon. I'm finding exercise to be a great way to manage the stress. Plus, it's good thinking time!

"It's just that there are so many obstacles to overcome. It's depressing."

"Obstacles like what?" she quizzes, sitting down next to me.

"Oh, things like raising start-up capital, developing marketing plans, creating corporate promotional materials, figuring out how to mass produce products, determining where to get supplies at the best prices - all that stuff." I show Annette my page long list of critical success factors - things I must do to overcome the forces against me and achieve my vision of success.

Critical Success Factors
- Need a detailed business plan with a rational strategy
- Need start-up financing and capital
- Need to legally incorporate the business
- Need corporate name and identity
- Need corporate bank account
- Need corporate marketing materials
- Need creative sales strategy
- Need competitive purchasing strategy
- Need to develop partnerships with quality vendors
- Need competitive pricing
- Need timely service
- Need efficient and prompt distribution system
- Need to manage time wisely and efficiently
- Need office machinery and supplies, computer, fax, phone, etc...
- Need part-time office assistance
- Need accounting systems and procedures
- Need a packaging plan
- Need packaging components and procedures
- Need a quality plan and procedures
- Need to understand customers' desires and habits
- Need positive and trusting relationships with stakeholders
- Need quality people to help out
- Need confidence
- Need energy and stamina
- Need credibility in the marketplace
- Need patience

"I can see how this might be a little overwhelming," she offers, looking over the list. "Perhaps that's why so many people give up?"

"Or go belly up," I add. "Carter says it's better for me to consider all of these things now, rather than after the fact. It's the only way to proceed rationally."

"Well, that certainly makes sense."

"And the workshop I went to earlier today really reinforced the importance of a clear business plan. It's amazing how detailed some of the people are in developing their strategies."

Annette smiles. "It's too bad you can't talk to Tom about this. I'll bet he could help you put together a terrific plan."

My mind races to my oldest son in New York. Annette's right. Tom knows this stuff inside and out. He could help immensely - if only he cared.

"I don't think Tom would have any interest in this," I mumble. "He's got problems of his own to worry about."

"So that's that?" Annette challenges. "You're not even going to try? How long are you going to go on believing that your son doesn't care about you?"

"I don't know. I just don't think this is the right time to approach him on something like this."

"What was it that Carter said to you that one day? Change your beliefs and you will change your outcomes? Isn't that what this is all about, Wayne? Don't you have to start challenging some of your old assumptions to reinvent yourself?"

Annette's right! I have made some very limiting assumptions in the past and it's unquestionably shackled my attitude and behavior. Perhaps this is why rational planning is so critical. It forces me to be more objective. It forces me to dissociate myself from my emotions and feelings and think more logically. All too often, I let my feelings cloud my judgement.

"Maybe this is what Walter was talking about when he said a lot of my competition has to do with my own internal belief system."

"Why don't you call Walter and ask him to go to New York with you to visit Tom? Isn't that what a proactive leader would do?" Annette stands up and walks over to the kitchen sink. She knows my hot buttons. She's read my guiding principles and my future biography and my ideal eulogy. She knows the direction I'm trying to go in. If I'm going to be principled, I have no choice but to do the right thing. And I've defined that as being proactive and responsible. As Walter puts it, "I have to step up to the plate."

"I suppose the worst I can do is strike out," I say.

"That's not much of a risk considering you also might hit a home run."

"Right now, I wouldn't mind just getting on base."

"That's the first step," says Annette as she opens the refrigerator door. "You want a glass of grapefruit juice?"

"Yeah, that sounds healthy," I reply, arching my back in my chair and stretching my arms over my head. I've been sitting for hours.

"So what are you going to call your company?" she asks.

I stand up and do a few knee bends. "I don't know," I gasp. "Right now, I'm thinking about Hopeless Endeavors."

Annette laughs. "I think you should name it after a bird. After all, birdhouses will be your specialty, won't they?"

"That and feeders," I add. "Maybe you're right. What's that one bird that always buries its head in the sand?"

Annette ignores my comment. "Tell me, what's your favorite kind of bird?"

I think for a moment. "I suppose an eagle. I know, why don't we name the company Baldies?"

My wife walks over to me and hands me my juice. "That's

one option," she says, kissing me on my balding head. "Let's try a few more."

After five minutes of brainstorming, we're at wit's end. We've explored everything from Birdbrain's to Hawkeye's to Cardinal Ideas. "I don't know, Nette. I kind of like Henpecker's," I chuckle.

Annette's not amused. "It's your company, Wayne. Call it whatever you want."

I sit back down in my chair. "You see what I mean. There are so many details to take care of. We can't even agree on a name."

Annette is gazing out the kitchen window. "You have to be patient. These things take time."

"I realize that. It's just so overwhelming." I lean forward and bang my head on the kitchen table."

Annette suddenly smiles as if she's got a brilliant idea. She turns and looks at me. "Do you believe in signs?"

"Signs? What signs?"

Without saying a word, Annette shuffles over and sits down next to me. Then she starts paraphrasing the Bible.

*"...do not worry about your livelihood, what you are to eat or drink or use for clothing... Look at the birds in the sky. They do not sow or reap... yet your heavenly Father feeds them... O weak in faith, will He not provide much more for you?"*

"What are you talking about?" I ask sharply.

"It's one of my favorite passages in the Bible - Matthew 6:26. We just discussed it in Bible class a few weeks ago."

"So why are you babbling about it now?"

Annette smiles. "Look out the window and tell me what you see?"

I turn and peer out the window wondering what Annette is talking about, only to discover a bright redheaded woodpecker looking straight at me. It seems this is the same woodpecker I saw the day Carter showed up with a chainsaw. Suddenly, the bird cocks his head to one side - as if trying to tell me something - and then returns to his work.

*"Woodpecker's,"* I whisper to myself. "That's good, Nette. It combines birds with wood. It's bright. It's colorful. It's perfect."

"I think it's a sign, Wayne. I think it's what you're meant to do."

I think back to what Carter said about purpose. You're serving your purpose in life when you are using your special gifts to benefit others.

"I think you're right, Nette. My purpose is to work with wood and create something that others can enjoy. I'm a wood-pecker."

She laughs. "Does this mean we can dress you up as a big, redheaded bird and send you out to the malls with a display of your products."

"Try again, Mother Hen. Maybe I'll put you in charge of mall sales."

Annette returns to a more serious tone. "Well, that raises another good point. Since I'm only working part-time at the law firm, I could help you with your office work. This is getting fun. Who knows? Perhaps someday you can hire me on full-time."

That's another great idea. Annette is an excellent legal secretary. She's a master at office administration, bookkeeping, word processing, you name it. This could work out beautifully.

"Would you consider that?" I ask sincerely.

"I'd love it. I think it would a wonderful stretch for both of us."

Wow! I haven't even finished listing my critical success factors and I can already check a few items off the list. Maybe this isn't impossible. Maybe it's time to start challenging some other assumptions.

# CHAPTER 17

U nlike his older brother, Walter promptly returns my phone calls. The message I left earlier in the day requested that he contact me at Woodpecker's. Annette and I have not formally requested the name yet, nor have we incorporated the business. I just want to test the new label out on my son. Surely, he recognizes our phone number.

"I think it's a great name, Dad! How did you come up with it?"

"Actually, your mother did all the creative thinking. I just served as the model."

"Well, congratulations! It sounds like you're making real progress."

I pause for a moment. "I'm trying, Son. But it sure feels like I've got a long, long way to go."

"Maybe that's because you haven't broken it down yet, Dad. You'll drive yourself nuts if you don't break your *macro* goals down into *micro* goals."

"That sounds like something my advisor said."

"I know I probably overuse this analogy, but think of it like playing a game of football. To compete effectively, you have to break the game down into manageable tasks - or micro goals. If you play the entire game thinking of nothing but the final score, you'll fail on every play because you won't be focused enough on the immediate task at hand. In football, we call these first downs. Golf is probably another useful metaphor. You have to break the game down into specific, measurable goals. Focus is critical. Anything worthwhile in life will seem overwhelming if you do not break it down into manageable units."

"So naming the company might be considered a first down," I comment.

"That's right. And hiring Mom just gained you a few more yards. Keep up the pace and you'll be on the scoreboard in no time."

"That's reassuring."

"Good. Just remember, every time you achieve a goal, you build momentum. That's why it's so important to set many, small, achievable goals that take you in the direction of your larger goals. The small ones stimulate a sense of possibility and generate an enormous source of power. Without them, the big ones will undoubtedly seem impossible.

As Walter speaks, my mind drifts to my other role model, Sam Walton. My son is right. Sam started with one store. Within a few years, he had his second. At one point, he dreamed off having five stores. Yet, by the time he died, he had hundreds all over the country. Talk about momentum.

My mind snaps back to the present. "Say, Walt, I wanted to ask you about our date with Tom. Have you had any luck setting something up?"

"As a matter of fact, I have. Tom's out of town all of this week, but he wants to come up to the Cape for Memorial Day weekend. How about if we rendezvous then?"

"That sounds great! Does he know I want to meet with him."

Walter pauses. "Yeah, he knows."

"You don't sound very excited."

"This is going to be difficult, Dad. Tom's pretty hurt."

"Hurt?" In all of my recent years, I've never heard that term used before to describe my eldest son. He always seemed like such a rock to me. "What do you mean by hurt?"

"You know, pained, cheated, victimized. He feels like you don't really care about him."

I'm tempted to defend myself and rationalize my behavior like I have in the past, but I don't. Instead, I change my direction and seek to understand. "Do you agree with that?"

"Let's just say I understand it, Dad. Tom never really felt like he had a father who cared about him as a person."

"But what about..." I start to interrupt.

"Hold on, Dad. Do you want to hear this or don't you?"

"You're right. I'm sorry. Go on."

"Think about it this way. Sure, you worked your ass off all day at TYPCO and put food on our table. You provided for us. That's a fact. It's also a given. Any father who brings life into this world and fails to take responsibility for it is no father in my mind. That's a responsibility every father has. Let's call that a reasonable standard of performance."

My son hesitates for a moment.

"Now, let's talk about exceptional performance - going *beyond* standard. This might include showing him new activities, taking him to exciting places, traveling the country together, attending important events in his life, building his self-esteem, helping him with his homework and just doing things together that a son dreams of doing with his father."

As Walter is speaking, my mind starts scanning the past twenty years. The truth is, when push came to shove, I let TYPCO take priority. Everything I did revolved around that company. How ironic. I give my life to a company and, at its convenience, it dumps me. I was motivated, but moving in the wrong direction. What a waste.

Worst of all, it cost me time with my family - time I can never get back. In many ways, Tom probably was a victim. Growing up, he never got the time or attention I gave to TYPCO or my workshop. He probably felt like a third wheel. We did things together at my convenience, not his. Perhaps, I was his TYPCO. I wonder how many other kids face the same situation. I'll bet Walter sees quite a few in his line of work. Maybe that's why he is so passionate about what he is doing. He's trying to make a difference.

"So how come this didn't affect you, Walt?" I ask after a brief silence.

"Two reasons, I suppose," he answers. "One, I'm not Tom. People react differently to similar circumstances. Maybe I tried to understand you a little more. I don't know."

"And the other reason?"

My son is direct. "I had Tom to look up to. He did many of the things for me that he probably wished you would have done for him."

Perhaps it's the way he says this, but it feels like Walter just reached in and ripped my heart out. My mind races to something Carter said about the value in mentors and role models. Who did Tom have to look up to - a hard-nosed, pessimistic man who had nothing positive to say about anything? If given a choice, would he have asked to assist me in the workshop while my mind was completely absorbed in what I was doing? Is this what the experts mean by spending quality time together?

"So do you think Tom is still hurting from his earlier years?" I ask.

"I don't know, Dad. I'm no psychotherapist, but given some of the things I've been reading about human behavior, I would guess that he has somehow neutralized himself from most of the experiences he's had with you. This is quite common for people going through separations."

"Even the good experiences?"

"I'm afraid so. Many times people try so hard to dissociate themselves from painful experiences that they end up dissociating themselves from the pleasant experiences, as well. They become the ultimate existentialist - the uninvolved observer - watching everyone else have fun but unable to experience any real fun for themselves."

"Now that you mention it, I remember hearing that mentioned on the NLP tape you loaned me. By neutralizing your feelings toward someone, you insulate yourself from future pain. Wow! I hope Tom hasn't neutralized me out of his life."

"I don't know, Dad. Right now, he seems so focused on his job that nothing else matters. I don't know how he feels about anything anymore."

"Well, what would you suggest I do to try to patch things up?"

"It's like I said before. Start with first downs. In this case, set a goal to open up communication. Write a letter. Try to build some empathy and understanding into the relationship. Think of it like going on a date for the first time. You can't take things too fast. Start with relatively simple, positive experiences. Focus on building a little momentum."

"I haven't written a personal letter in years."

"What difference does that make? You've got to look forward, not backwards, right?"

"Perhaps you're right. Maybe it is time for a change. Any other ideas?"

"Yeah," Walter says quietly. "Try praying."

My silence begs my son to continue.

"No matter how bad things might appear, no matter how much adversity you may face, you must always remember - you're never alone. Don't be afraid to ask for a little spiritual guidance from time to time. The act of faith is very powerful.

As Walter says this, I am reminded of people who appear to be pillars of strength in a world of pain and adversity. I think about those who have had their dreams dashed by some unpredicted setback, yet they move on with wisdom and understanding. I think about parents who have lost children, and children who have lost parents, yet they look to the future with promise and hope. I think about people who are mocked and scorned because they look different or act differently than the norm, yet they move forward with dignity and grace. Where do these people find the courage and strength to persevere? Is it that they never feel alone? Is it their faith that empowers them to move forward?

"I suppose I could use a little help from above," I mutter.

"Everyone can, Dad. Some people just don't know it yet."

"Thanks, Walt. I really appreciate your being straight with me."

"No problem. Hey, by the way, I have a lead for you on a possible supplier. Maybe this will help you pick up some more yardage."

I smile to myself. Walter's always thinking. "What's that?"

"Well, this friend of mine works at a small saw mill not far from you. I was telling him about your idea and he wants to talk to you. He says they have a lot of odd pieces of hardwood that they don't really have any use for. I guess it's excess wood from the cuts they make. It's too small to sell, and they don't want to attempt building anything with it. If you want, I'll give him your number."

I think immediately about my principle on being proactive. "How about if I take the lead on this one, Walt. Can you give me his number?"

Moments later, I'm looking at three new, micro goals scribbled on the paper in front of me.

*1. Write Tom*
*2. Say a prayer*
*3. Call Bruce Watkins at Crosscut, Inc.*

Surely, accomplishing these tasks doesn't seem too far out of reach. And I know they're productive actions because they move me in the direction I want to go. It's time to put the ball into play.

# CHAPTER 18

For what seems like hours, I sit and stare at the paper in front of me. It reads:

*Dear Tom,*

I think to myself - How do I begin a letter that may never even be read? How do I express myself honestly and sincerely without sounding like a failure? How do I admit my own shortcomings as a father without appearing to feel sorry for myself?

Finally, I decide to just start writing how I feel and forget all the rest. It's not like I'm entering any journalism contests.

> *I'm sorry. I know I've let you down. Of all the mistakes I've made in my life, my neglect toward you is clearly the most painful one of all. Only now do I realize the extent of my error.*
>
> *Recent events have opened my eyes to the many mistakes I've made - as an individual, as a manager, as a husband, and as a father. Unfortunately, I cannot go back in time and live my life over again. I can only learn from my errors and try to move forward with more wisdom, understanding and compassion.*

*I realize now that for many years, I abandoned the very people and activity that matter most in my life. Every year, I would make new promises to improve things. Then I would break these promises due to some urgency or conflict at work. Despite my good intentions, my priorities were clearly not in order. Now we both suffer.*

*I will understand if you choose never to forgive me. I have let you down, and I must bear responsibility for my neglect. I have made matters even worse by assuming that the responsibility and accountability belonged somewhere else. Now I know the truth, and I am truly sorry for the pain I have caused you.*

*You will always hold a special place in my heart - as my son and as an individual for whom I have great respect. It is I who am indebted to you for coming into my life and sharing all that you have shared. I only hope there is a small place left in your heart for me.*

*Love,*
*Dad*

As I reread the letter, I begin wondering what kind of reaction I will get. Will Tom go on ignoring me? Will he call? Will he return a letter? Perhaps I should mention our meeting on the Cape.

*P.S. I am very excited about meeting with you over Memorial Day weekend. How would you like to go fishing?*

As I envision Tom's face, I remember how much he used to like to go fishing as a boy. Every Saturday, he'd get up at the crack of dawn and head down to the local bait shop. Before you'd know it, he'd be home with a bucketful of something. Me? I never cared much for the sport. Maybe it's because I didn't have the patience of my oldest son. Or, maybe it's because I didn't have my priorities straight.

I address an envelope and seal the letter inside it. With my eyes closed, I stop for a moment and pray that my message gets through. Moving on in life without Tom, especially after realizing the pain I have caused him, just doesn't feel right.

Next, I dial up Bruce Watkins at Crosscut. Walter's timing couldn't have been better. If I'm going to succeed in this business, I have to have a solid relationship with a good wood supplier. Otherwise, there just isn't any sense in going forward. The big companies will eat me alive.

Seconds later, Bruce is on the line. He's the Operations Manager for the mill. "Hey, Mr. Peterson, I've been looking forward to talking with you. From what Walt's told me, your business concept may solve a problem we've had for years."

Ten minutes later, I'm convinced he's right. Apparently, some of the Grade A hardwoods coming out of the kiln are defective. This, coupled with unusual cut requirements, leaves the mill with fairly large quantities of good wood but in small, unusual sizes. Bruce explained that if I can get him detailed dimensions and order quantities, he could quote me some very competitive rates. I'm stunned. This could save me a fortune.

Bruce and I arrange a meeting for early next week and I promise to have detailed specs and order forecasts for him at that time. As Walter would put it, this has got to be about a forty yard dash down the sidelines. Wow! Now I'm beginning to understand why grown men spike the football and dance around in the endzone. What a great feeling!

Two minutes after hanging up the phone, it rings. Half expecting it to be Carter, I answer it, "Woodpecker's."

"Is Wayne Peterson there please?"

"This is Wayne," I reply, not recognizing the voice on the other end.

"Mr. Peterson, my name is Carla Danielson. I'm a friend of Walter's."

I smile. What is Walt up to now?

"Your son suggested that I contact you about an employment relationship. He told me about your business and I'm quite sure I can be of considerable help."

I think Walter's about three years ahead of me.

"Well, I appreciate your call, Carla. Unfortunately, I'm just getting the business started and I'm not really looking to hire anyone at the moment."

Carla laughs. "Oh, I'm not looking for a job, Mr. Peterson. I already have one. You see, I run a small outsourcing business. Our team consists of seventeen mentally and physically handicapped people. Your son Walter thought you might be able to use our service for some of your packaging needs. I understand you will have a lot of sorting to do."

"That's true," I admit, thinking now about how I'm going to get all of the screws and assembly components packaged for each ready-to-assemble product. "Unfortunately, I don't have much of a budget, Carla. In fact, I don't have any budget at all."

"Most of our clients don't, Mr. Peterson. That's one of the reasons they use us. Because we are mentally and physically challenged, we qualify for special assistance from the government. Plus, we have a van for all pick-ups and deliveries. I don't think you'll find a better financial arrangement anywhere. And I can assure you that you won't find a more dedicated and hardworking group of people. Why don't you think it over? I'll call back next week to follow up."

# CHAPTER 19

During the next three weeks, I make major gains. To begin with, I complete my business plan with detail I never even imagined. For example, I hammer out a win/win deal with Crosscut. They win because they now have a profitable use for their odd pieces of wood. I win because I now get my wood at a considerable value.

Carla has proven to be a saint. Her organization can package all of the screws and assembly components for my three different feeders and deliver them to me on a just-in-time basis. Her rates are very competitive and this allows me more time to work *on* my business system, not *in* my business system. Carter was right. I would have buried myself if I didn't understand this distinction.

I am also talking with a staffing firm about hiring temporary assistance to help me cut, shape, drill and package the wood. I have the equipment. All I need is someone to come in on a part-time basis and run it. By using temporary help, I don't have to put anyone on my payroll until I'm certain I can afford it. This saves me a lot of headaches associated with recruiting, hiring, worker's compensation, payroll taxes and the like. Instead of running a bureacracy, I can run an *adhocracy*. I use only what I need when I need it.

Given I set up a lean, productive, value-added system, I figure I can package approximately 2,000 ready-to-assemble products per month during my first year without any major investments in equipment or direct labor. At $30.00 per product, this gives me about $60,000 a month to work with, less overhead, operating expenses and material costs. All I have to do is figure out how to sell all the units we produce.

The beauty in providing people with ready-to-assemble products is two-fold. First, I am giving back. I am giving families an opportunity to build something together - something I could have done more of with my own two sons. This creates an experience that people can cherish forever. Second, I am avoiding a significant amount of manufacturing and finishing costs. By shifting the assembly work to the consumer, I can keep my overhead and operating expenses to a minimum.

Now, the challenge is coming up with an effective sales strategy. Joan, the ex-retailer in the workshop, has given me some useful tips on how to market my product to the big retailers. She's also helped me identify some small niche stores suitable for my products. At this point, I'm working up some sample proposals for her critique.

I'm also trying to contact an old classmate of mine who I understand owns a Birdwatcher's Unlimited franchise. Joan gave me his name and, as it turns out, we went to high school together. Birdwatcher's Unlimited is an operation of about 150 specialty bird stores nationwide. From what Joan tells me, it's ideal for my products.

I've also been casing out the giant retailers, and I've discovered that my prices are very competitive and that these products move very quickly - especially in the Spring and around Father's Day. My goal is to go after one giant retailer at a time.

I estimate my start-up costs to be minimal - despite the fact that some people are telling me to go out and borrow big bucks against the equity in my house. They suggest I invest the money in a lot of fancy equipment and office space and administrative help. Of course, a lot of these people have never run a business before, or they've run one into the ground. I prefer to start out as lean as possible.

Carter continues to provide me with invaluable insight. In fact, he suggests I subcontract everything I can to maximize my flexibility and keep my start-up costs low. He has also given me some excellent advice on how to negotiate win/win relationships with my vendors. For example, Crosscut is giving me net thirty day terms from the date of delivery. That means I have thirty days to sell the product before I have to pay for the wood.

Right now, I estimate my start-up costs to be about $12,000. This will cover my incorporation expenses, marketing materials, telephone lines, personal computer, fax, and two month's worth of packaging material. I do not plan to pay myself anything for the first six months of operation, and, after that, just a minimal amount to cover personal necessities. The only one at financial risk at this point is me. And with my severence package, I have the perfect opportunity to get started.

After laying out my entire operation schedule, there is no doubt in my mind that I can produce 2,000 products per month without any direct labor. Crosscut will supply the wood. Carla will package the assembly components. I will cut, shape, drill and package the products along with one or two temporary employees. And Annette will keep score.

The biggest question is - can I actually sell 24,000 bird feeders a year? And even if this is possible, how can I do it when I'm running the shop most of the day? It sure won't do me any good to produce something if I can't get rid of it.

I wonder what Tom would suggest. Since writing him three weeks ago, I haven't heard a word. I know we're still on for this weekend, but I don't want to turn this into a business discussion.

That's what destroyed our relationship in the first place. Yet, Tom knows so much about marketing and sales. If only he had an interest? I know he could help.

What if I just asked his opinion? What if I treated him as the expert? In years past, I was always the one doing all the talking and advising. Maybe it's time for me to do more listening?

On the other hand, what does Tom care? He probably doesn't expect any change in me. He's heard me make empty promises before. He probably took my letter and threw it away. I wonder if he'll even show up knowing I'm going to be there.

I know what I'll do. I'll call Walter and see if he's heard anything.

Midway through the third ring, Walter picks up the phone. "Hello?"

"Walter, it's Dad."

"Hi, Dad! What's up?"

"Well, I'm looking forward to this weekend and I'm trying to do some planning."

"What do you have in mind?"

"Well, first of all, do you know if Tom's still planning to come?"

"Yeah, I think so. I haven't heard anything to the contrary."

"Good. How would you guys like to charter a boat and go fishing?"

"Wow! That sounds like a great idea. It's kind of expensive, though."

"Don't worry about that. This is my treat."

Walter's voice is filled with enthusiasm. "Tom's going to love this. Does he know?"

"I don't think so. I never got any response to my letter."

Walter's sudden pause indicates he knows something.

"Have you heard anything, Walt?"

He is slow to respond. "Yeah, Tom called last weekend. He wanted to know how I felt about your coming for the weekend."

"And?"

"I told him I was excited about it. I told him the whole story about the changes you're making in your life and how you came down to visit me with your birdhouses and stuff. He seemed impressed."

"Did he mention my letter?"

"Yeah. He said he got a letter from you. He couldn't believe it. He thought maybe you were dying or something."

"Was he alarmed?"

Walter is direct. "No. Just curious."

"So you think fishing is a good idea?"

"Sure! I think it's a great idea! It's definitely a move that shows you are tuned into Tom's interests."

"What about getting a boat? Do you think we'll have any trouble getting a boat?"

"It probably wouldn't be a bad idea to reserve one. I'll tell you what, why don't you let me take care of the arrangements? I know someone who can probably help us out."

Walter's got to have more friends and contacts than anyone I know. His Rolodex must be huge. People are simply attracted to him. He's positive and optimistic. He has a healthy outlook on life. He's entertaining and fun. He's helpful and inspiring. People just feel good when they're with him. What a role model! Now all I have to do is figure out how to do the same thing myself.

# CHAPTER 20

A s I arrive at the marina, I see Walter standing on a dock waving. He's clad in a Hawaiian shirt and bright orange shorts. His eyes are covered by sleek sunglasses and he's got white sunscreen all over his nose. Tom is nowhere in sight.

I grab a cooler from the trunk of the car and head toward the boat.

"Ahoy!" yells Walter as I approach.

"Hey, Walt," I fire back. "This must be the place."

"This is it. Feast your eyes on this beauty - complete with captain and first mate, not to mention the latest in home appliances. All we have to do is fish."

"And pay for it," I mutter, looking over the 42-foot craft, *The Lady Kate*. "I was thinking of something a little bit smaller."

"Not to worry, Dad. Captain Jack here is giving us a special rate. All we have to do is pay for food and fuel."

"Pleased to meet you," Captain Jack yells from the bridge.

"Likewise," I volley back. "So how did you swing this, Walt?" I whisper.

"Captain Jack's son, Ben, and I teach school together. Ben's the first mate. He's in buying supplies. I help Ben and Captain Jack charter this boat over the summer."

"And what about Tom? Is he going to show up?"

"He's here. He just went down the street to the store."

I sigh a breath of relief. "Well, is there anything else we need?"

"Not a thing. Just jump aboard and make yourself at home."

Minutes later, I see Tom walking toward the boat. He's got a large box under one arm and a bottle in the other. He's smiling.

I stand to greet my son. "Hello, Tom."

Tom climbs aboard. "Hi." He sets the box down on a chair and extends his hand. "It's been a long time."

"It sure has," I reply. "Too long."

"Here," Tom hands me a bottle of expensive champagne. "It's to celebrate your new business."

"Thanks, Tom. Can I save it for after the boat ride?"

"I insist," he replies. "In fact, I thought maybe you and Mom might uncork it after your first order."

"That sounds like a great idea. Thank you."

"And this is for you, too." Tom reaches down and hands me the box.

"Wow! What is this?" I say, opening the box. Inside is a beautiful engraved plaque that reads *Woodpecker's, Incorporated 1995*. "It's fantastic!"

"Well, I'm proud of you. It's good to see you doing what you enjoy."

Tom remains poised and stoic. I feel like hugging him, but I don't think the timing's right. I remember Walter suggesting that I treat this like a first date. We have a lot of rebuilding to do.

"Here comes Ben," Walt shouts. "What do you say we do some fishing, boys?"

Soon after a quick round of introductions, Captain Jack has *The Lady Kate* moving slowly out of the marina. It's a gorgeous day, 75 degrees Fahrenheit, sunny with a few clouds, 10 to 15 knot winds out of the Southwest, waves one to three feet. People are lining the pier to catch a glimpse of the beautiful boats cruising by and we're fortunate enough to be on one. The beaches are already packed.

Walter and Ben are busy preparing the bait and fishing equipment and Captain Jack is steady at the wheel. Tom and I are sitting on swivel chairs at the stern of the boat.

After a long silence, Tom asks, "So are you glad to be out of TYPCO?"

"I am, Tom. At first, I was pretty bitter. You know, I felt like I was cheated. But now? Now I see the light."

"Do you ever talk to Jack MacDonald anymore?"

"Nope. Haven't talked to him since I left."

"Do you miss his friendship?"

Tom's question catches me by surprise. "What do you mean?"

"Well, you guys used to be pretty good friends, didn't you?"

"Yeah, we were pretty tight."

"And now that's over?"

My first instinct is to defend myself. The man fired me for crying out loud. What do you expect? But then my inner voice reminds me to slow down and manage the gap between stimulus and response. I have a choice in how I respond.

"I guess I haven't given it much thought," I say.

"So what prompted your letter to me?" Tom asks.

I look at him. He's looking past me to the ocean, his eyes hidden behind his dark sunglasses. "I miss you."

He says nothing.

"And I want you to know how I feel."

He's still looking away. "I thought you were dying or something."

I speak softly. "Maybe I was."

Tom glances over at me. "What do you mean?"

I swivel my chair so that I'm facing him. "Would you believe that I've lost 15 pounds in the past six weeks?"

"You look good."

"And I'm walking between ten and fifteen miles per week now?"

Tom nods his head. "I'm impressed."

"I'm not saying this to impress you. I'm only telling you this because three months ago, I was in serious trouble. I didn't know what I wanted. I had no direction in my life. I was a walking time bomb."

"So what happened?"

"I changed the way I look at things. Rather than blame outside forces like I have in the past, I'm now taking responsibility for my outcomes. I'm looking inward for the answers."

"Are you happier?"

"I'm more at peace. I have a long way to go before I can say I feel happy and secure, but I'm beginning to understand that security and certainty are nothing but illusions. Chasing them makes no sense. Instead, I'm learning to see the value and excitement of uncertainty. I'm testing myself and building more inner strength. I feel better about myself - like I'm getting my dignity and honor back. I feel so much more alive."

"I'm happy for you."

Walter was right. Tom is definitely neutral about things. It's as if he's speaking to a stranger on the street. Our connection as father and son has disintigrated.

"What about you? Are you happy in New York?"

The young man swivels back and forth in his chair. "Not really. I mean, there's a lot of advantages. I'm paid well. There's a million things to do. I travel to interesting places. I meet a lot of interesting people. But it's getting kind of old."

"Dating anybody?"

"No one in particular." He pauses. "Well, there is one girl I'm starting to see a lot of."

"Is she from New York?"

"No, actually she's from Rhode Island, but she comes down to New York a lot on the weekends."

"How did you meet?"

He laughs. "It's a long story. Let's just say we met at a party - a New Year's Eve party."

"What's her name?"

Tom smiles. "Kelsey."

For the next fifteen minutes, our dialogue continues like that of two strangers waiting at a bus stop. Finally, I ask a question that really gets Tom's attention. It's a question Carter used to open me up.

"So what do you dream about, Tom?"

He hesitates for a minute. "I don't know. I guess I dream about work. No, that's not right. I used to dream about work. Now I dream about getting out of New York, maybe starting a business of my own. I think about getting married, starting a family, taking my kids fishing." He pauses for a moment. "I suppose I dream about all the things I want in life that I don't have now."

"Really? That surprises me. I thought you were happy in New York."

"Don't get me wrong. I wouldn't trade my experience in New York for anything. I've had a great time, and I've learned a lot. But I suppose I'm in the same predicament you were in at TYPCO. I've been working my ass off but I haven't really defined my direction in life."

"Do you know where you want to go?"

"I guess I haven't really given it much thought. I spend so much time working, I don't think about what it's leading to."

"Yet, your dreams are starting to steer you away from New York?"

"Yeah, that's true."

"What about your moments of bliss? What kinds of things give you the most satisfaction in life?"

Tom laughs. "My moments of bliss?"

"Yeah. It's a term my outplacement advisor uses. He's a real character."

Tom continues laughing. His laugh is hearty. "Oh, I suppose fishing is one of them, although I never have much time for it anymore."

"What is it about fishing you like so much?" I ask, probing to unlock the source of Tom's true passion.

"Hmmm. I guess I love the challenge of seeing what I can catch. Maybe that's why I like advertising and marketing so much. It's a lot like fishing. You have to think of ways to catch people's attention."

"So for you, a moment of bliss in business might be using your special talents to come up with creative ways to hook a customer?"

"Yeah, exactly. I love thinking of unique ways to attract people to buy a product."

I smile. It's now or never. "Do you think you could convince 24,000 people to buy birdfeeders every year?"

Tom laughs. "What is that supposed to mean?"

"It means I can produce 24,000 ready-to-assemble birdfeeders a year, but I don't know how to get rid of them."

"I hope you don't have them piling up in your garage."

"No, not at all. In fact, I'm not even officially in business yet. I'm still putting the plan together. But I'm serious about the production. I can produce and package over 2,000 ready-to-assemble products per month."

"Wow! Are you sure about that?"

"I'm positive. I can show you the plan."

"And you can finance it?"

"I've got enough to get started. It's all covered in my plan. The only thing missing now is the marketing piece. And I'm not going into business until I'm confident about that piece."

"Do you have a marketing budget?"

"Not really. Just enough to cover initial corporate identity materials and the like. I can't really afford to do much advertising, and the banks I've talked to so far won't lend me a dime without collateral. Evidently, they don't like start-up companies."

"That sounds about right."

"But I'm not going to let that stop me. I have enough resources to get started on my own as long as I'm careful about how I invest it."

"Have you identified your primary market?"

"Yep." Minutes later, Tom is in his glory. He's got leads with some of the buyers at the big retailers. He's got marketing slogans. He's got catalogue ideas. He's got radio jingles. He's got Woodpecker's selling all over North America.

"24,000 per year? No problem. The trick, of course, is to get the fish to come to you. It's just like fishing. You can't possibly jump in the sea and catch all the fish by yourself - especially with your budget. You have to come up with creative ways to bring attention to yourself. Your product is wonderful. Selling it as a family 'do-it-yourself' project is another attractive feature. It's also a great gift item. In fact, we could probably list twenty different positive features about it right now. This is what you have to market. *You market the benefits, not the product.*"

"Would you ever consider helping me with it? I'll pay you whatever I can."

Tom suddenly returns to his stoic self. The excited child he so briefly revealed has retreated to his room. "I'm not interested in your money, Dad. But I'll do what I can to help."

This is the first time Tom has called me Dad in two years. "I hope I didn't insult you. I just want to offer you what I can."

"That's where you're wrong, Dad. There's only one thing I've ever really wanted from you and it isn't your money."

Tom doesn't need to explain any further. It's written in his eyes. My son wants a father.

---

"Are you boys ready to fish?" Walter steps between us and shoves a fishing pole into each of our hands. "It's time to start reelin' 'em in!"

Tom's boyish grin returns. My son is back in his glory.

# PART V

## Confront Your Fears

"Satisfaction lies in the effort, not in the attainment.
Full effort is full victory."
*Mohandas Gandhi*

# CHAPTER 21

"How was your weekend?" Annette greets me at the door with a giant smile. Her eyes are sparkling.

"Excellent!" I reply, dropping my bags in the front hall and giving her a big hug. "I couldn't have asked for a more revitalizing weekend."

Annette starts leading me toward the kitchen when suddenly I remember something in the car.

"Hold on. I have to get something."

Minutes later, I return with Tom's plaque and the bottle of champagne. "These are from Tom."

"Oh, how thoughtful," she says. "And you didn't think he cared."

"You know what's amazing, Nette? Tom is going through the same thought process I'm going through."

"What do you mean?" Annette looks up from the plaque.

"He's confused. He likes what he's doing, and he's doing it well, but he's starting to question where it's taking him. He's starting to wonder about his own direction in life."

"Maybe you can help?"

"I think I already have. I started telling him about some of the visioning exercises Carter has had me working on - you know, preparing my own personal mission statement, drafting my future biography, writing my own eulogy, defining my guiding principles, all that stuff - and he was really into it. He said it was the kind of thing he never learned in school."

"Perhaps that's something parents should be teaching their children on a more regular basis."

"I'm sure it is. But how are we supposed to teach something we don't really understand ourselves?"

"Good question. Maybe that's why there are so many unhappy people in the world. We often have the blind leading the blind."

"Anyway, we had a great time. Tom is still very neutral towards me, and I can't blame him. But we opened up the lines of communication and I feel like I'm finally renewing our relationship as father and son."

"So your assumptions about Tom were wrong."

"My assumptions about a lot of things have been wrong. My assumptions about myself, my assumptions about my dreams, my assumptions about my sons, my assumptions about Jack MacDonald - all of these assumptions have restricted my growth and prosperity. If there's one thing I've learned through all of this, it's to challenge my internal beliefs."

"You are a new man, Wayne. No, let me correct that. You're more like the man I met thirty-one years ago - a man with energy and passion."

"And now you can add purpose and character to that."

Annette smiles. "I love you just the same."

"You know, that's what amazes me. How come you never gave up on me?"

My wife turns and looks me in the eyes. "Because you're part of my purpose in life. We were meant to be, Wayne, and I'm committed to that."

Wow. I never thought of it like that. Annette's had this figured out all along. She knows her mission in life and she uses it to set her priorities. She's given birth to two remarkable boys. She's nurtured them to achieve great accomplishments. She's stood by my side through thick and thin. She's kept this family together, despite my obnoxious behavior. And now she's prepared to assist me with what might prove to be my craziest idea yet.

"You're fantastic, Nette. Maybe you should lead this company."

"No. My purpose is to serve, not to lead."

I suddenly remember something Jack MacDonald said. "Aren't they one in the same?"

Annette pauses to think. "Perhaps they are. Maybe we should lead the new company together?"

"That sounds like a wise approach. We can both serve the business."

"Speaking of business, did you catch any fish?"

"We caught a boatload. I'll tell you what, when it comes to reeling in the fish, Tom and Walt really know what they're doing. I never realized fishing could be so much fun."

Annette grabs me by the hand and pulls me toward the kitchen. "Well, I have a little surprise for you, too."

As we enter the kitchen, I see a beautiful leather desk set on the table, complete with an engraved pen and pencil set. "It's for our corporate headquarters."

I walk over to the table and sit down in front of it. "It's gorgeous, Nette. Thank you."

She smiles. "You deserve the very best, Wayne. Now, it's time to incorporate."

I look up at her from the table. "Are you sure?"

"I'm positive. What's the worst thing that can happen?"

"We could lose our start-up investment. That's about $12,000!

"And what's the best thing that can happen?"

I smile. "We can achieve our vision of success. We can give families something to do together all over the country. We can sell millions of birdfeeders and ready-to-assemble crafts. We can eventually travel the world teaching others how to reinvent themselves and turn their dreams into realities." I laugh. "Or, we can die trying."

"Does that scare you, Wayne?"

"Not as much as it used to. This whole planning process has really helped me understand how to make it work. Don't get me wrong. I'm still nervous. But I'm sure we can make it work - especially with Tom's marketing help."

Annette looks directly at me. "And he's willing to help?"

"He said he'll do whatever he can. In fact, he's already sending me the names of a couple of buyers for a big retailer he works with."

"And what if I went to work full-time at the law firm for the next twelve months to help us through the start-up period? Would you be opposed to that?"

"You don't need to do that, Nette."

"But what if I want to? The added income will certainly be useful."

"I suppose we are going to need all the financial help we can get."

"Then it's settled. I'll go back to work full-time and help you out at night and on weekends. That puts me at financial risk, too."

I stand up and hug Annette. What a saint!

"Should we crack open that bottle of champagne?" she whispers.

"Not yet," I reply. "Tom wants us to save that for our first order."

"Ooh. That's going to require some discipline."

"What is? Waiting for the champagne or getting our first

order?"

Annette laughs. "Both, I suppose. But then, we shouldn't even consider going into business if we can't exercise patience and self-discipline."

Just like fishing, I think to myself. Perhaps this will be more fun than I thought.

# CHAPTER 22

After doing all the preliminary planning, Annette and I agree to take the risk. Carter and Walter were right. By breaking the process down into manageable units, I have been able to see very clearly what I must do in order to succeed. And either way, I will never have to ask myself the question 'What if I had taken the risk?' I will never have to live with the regret of not trying.

Annette puts me in touch with a lawyer at her firm and we fully incorporate under the name *Woodpecker's, Inc.*. I buy the first 2000 shares of stock at $1.00 per share. I then open a corporate bank account at my local bank with the $2,000 investment amount along with a personal loan from me to the company for $10,000.00. I also apply for a corporate credit card and I open a business account at Builder's Paradise and Office Mania. This gives me plenty of working capital to get started.

Annette finds a free lance CPA to serve as our accountant and auditor. Annette will keep the day-to-day books and handle all of the monthly tax requirements, in addition to working full-time at the law firm. Claudia, the CPA, will take care of the rest.

Joe, the outplaced designer, is working up some sketches for me on my corporate identity. As soon as he is finished, I will send them on to Tom for his feedback. Once Annette and I choose one, we'll move forward with all of our marketing materials. I figure another six to eight weeks and we'll be up and running.

Joe is also helping me with my visual assembly procedures. He suggested that I put the assembly diagram and instructions right on the box. This shows the consumer how easy it is to assemble as part of the buying decision. By next week, I should have the artwork completed for all three product packages.

Annette has equipped our corporate headquarters with only the most necessary equipment - a phone, a fax and a personal computer. She is training me on how to use the various software programs she purchased, but I am leaving most of the administrative details to her. My time is better spent concentrating on activities that give Annette numbers to compute. That means I'm dedicating the majority of my time to marketing and setting up an efficient production operation.

Our goal for June is to produce and package only 300 birdfeeders - 100 of each type. This keeps our inventory and material costs down and gives us samples to use in our marketing campaign. We now have color pictures of each finished product for our brochure.

Tom and Joan have both given me the names of several people in the retail trade, and I have four meetings scheduled to explore possibilities with them. I'm also meeting later this week with Daniel Post, that high school classmate of mine who owns several Birdwatchers Unlimited stores.

Tom helped me work up a short presentation, but he reminded me that the best thing to do in an introductory meeting is to ask questions and gather information. He said I should focus on figuring out what the prospect's primary objectives are and what their points of dissatisfaction are. Once I'm armed with this information, I can tailor my proposal to help them solve their problems. Tom always reminds me that I'm selling benefits and solutions, not birdfeeders.

Carter has also proven to be a wise and loyal advisor. He has given me countless leads on where to find useful information and resources. I never realized it before, but everything a person could ever need to run a successful business is all around them. The trick is knowing how to find the resources and put them to use. Libraries, bookstores, specialty stores, large retailers, merchants, people, banks, associations, chambers of commerce, you name it - they're all right there. I just never took the time to pay any attention.

I still have to face my fears everyday. I worry about losing my investment. I worry about humiliating myself. I worry about getting in over my head - perhaps losing my house, maybe even my retirement savings. And if I do fail, I worry about not being able to get another job. After all, who wants to hire a failure? But, as Walter puts it, you're never a failure if you've given it your best shot. You're only a failure if you don't have the guts to step up to the plate. I have a feeling I'm going to be whiffing for awhile. Living with uncertainty has never been easy for me.

Whenever I start getting depressed, I think about my sensory vision of success. Carter said as long as I stay focused on who I want to become and what I want to achieve, I will find the strength to overcome any adversity along the way. But this vision of success has to be vivid and real. It has to stimulate my senses. It has to be bright and colorful, and I have to learn to fade any negative images of myself into the darkness. I have to see myself everyday as the person I want to become, not as the person I am now or the person I was in the past. I have to "reprogram my internal software" and stick with it.

I am also learning to spend a little time each day meditating and praying. Walter was right. This, coupled with a strong sense of purpose and direction, generates a very powerful force inside of me. I am starting to appreciate that I am not alone.

My most pressing fear right now is this meeting I have tomorrow with Mega-Mart. One order from this place and I could be busy for years. Joan gave me the lead, and Tom has given me some helpful insights. Still, I can't seem to shake the anxiety. Sometimes I wonder what I'm getting myself into. Maybe I should call that recruiter back and tell him I'm interested in going back into plant management. Or maybe I should just go out to the shop and build a new prototype to relieve a little stress. No, that's what Carter cautioned me not to do. I've got to give this my total commitment. And I've got to work *on* the system. I can't afford to bury myself inside it.

I wonder if Tom gets this nervous before a big meeting. Maybe I should try calling him. I pick up the phone and start dialing.

# CHAPTER 23

The three minutes I remain on hold seem like an eternity. Is this just a creative way to screen my call? Is Tom trying to get me to hang up? Check your assumptions, Wayne. He's probably just busy.

"Hey, Dad, thanks for waiting. My boss was just coming down on me about another crisis we're facing. Sometimes it never ends."

"Well, I don't want to interfere, Tom. I just wanted your opinion on something."

"Shoot. I'm listening."

"I've got this big meeting tomorrow with the buyer from Mega-Mart. I believe I told you about it last week."

"Yeah, I remember."

I hesitate for a few seconds to think about what I'm about to say. This is the first time I will be openly admitting to my oldest son that I am not the pillar of strength I've been pretending to be. The truth is, I'm scared! I take a deep breath. "Anyway, I guess I'm a little worried about it. I'm not really sure I'm ready for this."

Tom pauses. "It sounds like you're afraid to succeed, Dad."

His comment catches me by surprise. "What do you mean?"

"Well, I know you're not afraid to fail. Otherwise, you never would have come this far. I'll bet you're afraid to succeed."

"I still don't understand what you're talking about."

"This goes beyond your comfort level. You're more comfortable chipping away on a small project in your shop. This is the big league, Dad. If you get a hit here, you're in a whole new zone!"

"And you think I'm afraid of that?"

"It's not a big deal, Dad. Most people prefer to stay in their own comfort zones. They choose to play it safe. They hold themselves back. You, on the other hand, have decided to stretch. You've designed a business plan to take you to a new level."

"And now it's gametime."

"That's right. And that tends to make people nervous. But there's nothing wrong with that. In fact, it's good. Getting nervous before a performance means you care. It means you want to do a great job. It also gets your heart pumping and your blood circulating. This prepares you physically, as well as emotionally. You must learn to embrace this feeling, not avoid it."

"That's assuming I don't have a heart attack in the lobby."

Tom laughs. "You've already taken some excellent steps to avoid that. Now it's time to step out onto the stage and perform. This is your chance to reel people in. Just remember, you'll never catch any fish if you don't put your line in the water."

"That sounds like something your brother said." I wonder if this is one of those things Walter learned from his older brother.

"Well, it's true, Dad. Unfortunately, you fear that you won't be able to handle the success. You're afraid that if you catch a whopper, it's going to pull you under."

"So that's what you mean by fear of success."

"That's right. Some people prefer to stay on the sidelines and cheer. They don't dare get into the game. Or they don't think they deserve to. It's safer to watch and critique those who take the risks in life."

Tom is right. I don't really know what I'm capable of because

I've never really put myself on the line. I've played it safe. I've gone the secure route. Now, I'm being tested. Wow! I wonder what I can really do.

"I suppose now is the time to find out what I'm really capable of," I say.

"That's right, Dad. It's gametime!"

"Any advice on how to handle the meeting?"

"Just focus on the stated desires of Mega-Mart. Try to find ways where you can help create an opportunity for them - or solve a problem. Ask good questions and, more importantly, make a good first impression. It's the one thing you can never do over again."

"Right."

"And don't try to accomplish everything in one meeting. Use this meeting for information gathering and fact-finding. You can then come back with a more sensible proposal focusing on what *they* want, not just what you want."

"Good idea."

"Oh, and one more thing," he continues.

"Yeah?"

*"Don't forget to listen."*

# CHAPTER 24

**M**y meeting with Mega-Mart went pretty much as expected. I got some very useful information about their procurement system, their specific objectives, and their current points of disatisfaction.

For starters, they want just-in-time delivery within 48 hours of order and their order quantities must be met in full - no shortages. They expect zero-defects, which is their biggest complaint problem now, especially with ready-to-assemble products. And they rarely give second chances.

No wonder Tom suggested that I shoot for a second meeting. I would have blown myself right out of the water if I had tried to use the traditional "close close close" sales approach. These people are looking for trusted partners, not "here today, gone tomorrow" salespeople.

By the end of the meeting, I had more than enough information to conclude one thing. I'm not ready for this league.

The two buyers I met with seemed pleased with my honesty and they invited me back for a second meeting in six months. They loved my products and were impressed by my deliberate planning. My shortcomings were primarily a result of my infancy in business. Once my business system is running smoothly, I'll be in position to serve Mega-Mart on mutually beneficial terms.

The other three meetings I had with the big retailers were

essentially the same. The good news is, I learned a lot about their purschasing systems, their objectives and their points of dissatisfaction. The bad news is, Annette and I haven't opened the champagne yet.

It is becoming increasingly clear to me at this point that the only way I can meet the big retailers demands is by building a sizable inventory of finished goods. Unfortunately, I don't have the capital to finance that much manufacturing. Well, that's not entirely true. I could take out a business loan secured by the equity I have in my home. I could also tap into my retirement fund. But I don't think I'm ready for that much risk. What if I built an inventory of 10,000 birdfeeders and no one wanted them? I'd be broke. On the other hand, if I don't sell at least 1000 birdfeeders a month, I'll go broke.

My meeting with Daniel Post should be interesting. If nothing else, it will give me a contrast between the big retailers and the smaller, niche franchises. Daniel owns nine New England stores, three in Massachusetts, two in New Hampshire, two in Vermont, and one in Maine and Rhode Island. Evidently, he's doing very well.

As I pull into the parking lot of his main store, I immediately notice something peculiar. The design of his store looks a lot like the design of one of my birdfeeders. It's a simple, rustic design - rectangular with a pitched roof, stained wood - very earthy.

I remember Daniel when we were in high school together. We didn't really know each other very well. In fact, I don't think anyone knew Daniel very well. He was kind of a loner - always off in dreamland somewhere. But somehow he must have found his niche.

The next thing I notice when I enter the store is the uniqueness of it. It's a bird lover's paradise. The shelves are stocked with everything you could imagine dealing with wild birds - books, binoculars, clothing, hats, jackets, pictures, you name it! There must be 500 different items.

My eyes race immediately for birdfeeders and birdhouses. There are a few, but they're all preassembled and all but two of them are made out of plastic. Daniel's also got a healthy stock of birdbaths and birdfeed, but I don't see anything like my designs.

After strolling through each aisle in the small store, I head up the staircase to the second floor where Daniel's offices are. I am greeted at the top of the stairs by a man I probably never would have recognized. Daniel Post has transformed himself from a skinny little runt in high school to a modern day Paul Bunyon. He stands about six feet tall. He's got a solid build and he now wears a salty beard. He's dressed in a red plaid flannel shirt, jeans and suspenders. Only his eyes seem to be the same.

"Wayne Peterson! What's it been? Thirty years?" he growls.

"Longer than that, I suspect," comes my reply.

"Well, C'mon in and sit down."

As we enter his office, a middle-aged woman stands to greet me.

"This is my wife, Marsha, Wayne. She runs the business with me."

"Hi, Marsha. It's nice to meet you."

"Likewise," she says, shaking my hand. "Daniel tells me some interesting tales about you in high school."

"I'll bet he does," I reply. "I was sure pushing the limits back then."

Twenty minutes later, Daniel and Marsha have heard my life's story and I've heard theirs. What amazes me most is that this quiet, simple man who everyone perceived as a daydreamer in high school followed his dreams as well as anyone I've ever known. After high school, Daniel went on to college for two and a half years. Then, much to his parent's dissatisfaction, he dropped out of school to work for an entreprenuer who was running a specialty gardening shop.

He met Marsha while he was working at the specialty shop and two years later they were married. Both of them have a passion for birdwatching and, therefore, it wasn't long before they convinced their mentor to include wild bird paraphernalia in the store. Years later, they bought the store from its founder and developed it into what it is today. Ten years ago, Daniel hooked up with Birdwatchers Unlimited and his nine stores are now part of a national franchise of over 150 stores.

"So why did you hook up with Birdwatchers Unlimited?" I ask.

"They made us a win/win offer," he says calmly. "Now we have access to more products at better prices. We have a substantial increase in catalogue sales. We still maintain ownership and rights over the New England territory. And our name is recognized all over the country. We're on the map, so to speak."

"I see." My mind drifts to Tom's boyish grin. Get the fish to chase you, Dad.

"Can I get a copy of your catalogue?" I ask curiously.

"Absolutely," Marsha says, standing up to get one. Minutes later, I'm leafing through a beautiful color catalogue of everything you can imagine that might be of interest to outdoor lovers and bird enthusiasts.

"Wow! How often does this come out?" I ask.

"Twice a year," Daniel says. "Spring and Fall."

My mind races to some of Tom's comments about creative ways to advertise without any money. "Can I ask what I would have to do to get pictures of my birdfeeders into this catalogue?"

Daniel laughs. "Yeah. Get me a few of your products and let me see if they sell."

"That's it?" I ask.

"That's how Marsha and I handle our research and development. We just put quality stuff on our shelves and give it eight weeks. If it sells, we'll cut you a check. If it doesn't, we'll return it to you."

Now I understand why Daniel had so much trouble paying attention in school. He was probably bored stiff with all the textbook theory and analysis.

"That sounds fairly simple. How about if I drop off three different models along with one assembled model of each for display? Will you have room for that?"

"We'll make room," Daniel says. "Judging from the pictures you sent me, your products should do very well here. And if they do, we'll get you into our Fall catalogue."

"Can I ask what the circulation is on the catalogue?"

"All together, about 20,000 catalogues go out through direct mail. About another five thousand are distributed through the stores."

"Wow! That's a pretty impressive mailing list."

"You just have to make sure you can deliver. We don't like to keep our customers waiting for something they want now. Do you see this as a problem?"

"Not unless you want more than 3,000 a month," I reply. "And if that's the case, I'll make sure you get them within two weeks."

Daniel laughs. "It sounds like you have the production end covered."

"That's what I've spent the past twenty years doing, Daniel. Trust me, if you can sell these things, I can make them and deliver them on time."

"Well, let's give it a shot," Daniel says, standing up and extending his hand.

"I'll have my products here on Monday," I reply, shaking

hands. "Thanks for giving me the opportunity to work with you."

As I leave the store, I think back to the young Daniel Post I knew in high school. How ignorant I was. The last thing anyone would have said to describe Daniel was that he was a leader. Yet he had a vision and he had the guts and the self-discipline and the passion to pursue that vision. What more does it take to lead an enriching life?

# CHAPTER 25

The three pre-assembled models I will deliver to Daniel next week glisten on my workshop bench. The first one mirrors Daniel's store. I used an identical mahogany stain to finish it and the brass trimmings accent it with a touch of class. The second model is pure white - just for contrast. I decide to leave the third model unfinished. This is to show how each model will look in terms of color when it is assembled. It will be up to the consumer to determine how to finish it.

My box designs look great. The instructions are relatively simple. There are diagrams to show how the finished product should look. My Woodpecker name and logo are fantastic. And the color scheme is magnificent. Joe might not know how to run a business, but he sure knows his trade. I wonder if Carter ever explained the difference between working on your system and working in your system to Joe.

I still can't get over the remarkable accomplishments of Daniel Post. I mean, this guy could have clearly won the title "Most Likely to Fail" in high school. Yet, somehow he knew what he wanted and he went after it. How ironic! Some of the kids in high school who always seemed to be at the head of the class are probably the most unhappy. They got the college degree. They got the masters degree. They got the big titles and high paying jobs. But are they passionate about what they're doing? Are they really following their dreams?

And then there's Daniel. If I didn't know better, I'd probably think the guy works in a lumberyard. Yet, he's got to be worth millions. And that doesn't even seem to matter to him. He's doing what he loves and he's got the money chasing him. How many people have that backwards? How many people spend their whole lives chasing money, only to discover that with that mind-set, there is never enough?

Maybe that's what I've got to learn to do. When I think back, I've always spent my time doing things I felt I had to do to earn a living. And look where that's gotten me - unemployed with regret. Perhaps it's time I start chasing my passion rather than my pension. But do I really trust that the money will follow? I can't afford to chase my dreams into bankruptcy. The temptation to play it safe is powerful.

I look around my shop. Not much has really changed externally - at least, not yet. Everything is still exactly where it was three months ago when I first met Carter Johnston. My cabinets still aren't finished. My desk is still just an idea in my head. My shop is still just a shop.

But internally, there is no doubt I have changed. My focus has changed. My energy level has changed. My relationships have changed. My physical body has changed. I've now lost twenty-two pounds. My whole outlook on life has changed. I no longer find it necessary to sit around and complain about everything that's wrong with the world. Instead, I now spend my time concentrating on the things I can change myself.

But for some reason, I still feel like I'm holding back. As much as I've tried to change my core assumptions and beliefs, I still have a lot of self-doubt. Maybe I am afraid to succeed. Perhaps Tom is right. Or maybe I don't think I deserve it. I don't know. I guess my self-esteem isn't what I thought it was. I'm my own worst enemy.

My mind returns to Daniel. Somehow, he never seemed to concern himself with what everyone else thought of him. He was ridiculed and he knew it. He was harassed, but he never let it get under his skin. He was almost disowned by his own parents when he dropped out of college, but he persevered. He was broke when he got married, but he tells his story with passion and romance. The man obviously swam upstream most of his life. While everyone else was gliding with the current, there was Daniel dodging them all. I suppose, if nothing else, he was focused. He knew what he wanted, and no one was going to move him off course.

Walter's done the same thing. Despite the many adversities he's faced, he has always remained focused. When Walter runs into an obstacle, he finds his way around it. He improvises. He resets his goals. He just keeps moving forward. His life will be fascinating to watch because he understands the principles of success so well and he is committed to lifelong learning. Today, he is a teacher influencing the lives of hundreds of kids. Who knows? Tomorrow he may be teaching millions more using another format.

And what about Carter? From day one, this man has impressed me as being clearly different - another fish swimming upstream. He has passion for his work just like Daniel and Walter. You can see it in his eyes. You can feel it when you listen to the man speak. He knows he can make a difference and he's doing it. I shudder to think where I might be if Carter had not intervened. Yet, I'm sure Carter has had his adversities to overcome. I'm sure he's had to struggle against the current.

So what am I to do? I've defined my mission and my guiding principles. I've developed a vehicle and a plan for getting there. I know what I want to achieve and who I want to become, but it's all upstream. The current is against me. My dreams are upstream. Victory is upstream. But the forces to go with the flow and be like everyone else are powerful. I still get calls every now and then from that recruiter tempting me to go back into plant management. He starts quoting me big dollar figures and telling me how foolish it is at my age to start dabbling in a risky entrepreneurial venture. "Play it safe," he says. "You're not that far away from retirement. You can always pursue your dreams after that."

By the sounds of it, he already has me doing better financially at a new company than I was at TYPCO. He's selling me like I'm some kind of priceless jewel. Yet the man has never even met me. He doesn't know who I am or what I'm capable of. The more I think about it, the more I wonder if he even cares.

I guess if I'm going to achieve the kind of satisfaction and success that my role models have achieved, I'm going to have to follow through. I'm going to have to give this my *total commitment*. I'm going to have to plug myself in - no more holding back.

# PART VI

# Plug Yourself In

"Boldly begin your dream."
*Goethe*

# CHAPTER 26

Carter relaxes in his chair. His hands are clasped in front of his chin and he is looking to the ceiling as if deep in thought.

"How did I get into this field?" he repeats. "That's a good question, Wayne."

I sit silently on the other side of his desk.

"Well, it all started when I got fired from my job. I suppose I felt a lot like you did the day we met."

My eyebrows leap to the top of my head. I never would have guessed Carter had been fired.

"Unfortunately, my boss didn't have the compassion and insight that your former boss had, and I was out on the street with no help at all. To tell you the truth, it almost destroyed me. My wife was pregnant with our second child. She was not employed. We had no savings to speak of. And I was caught totally by surprise."

"You had no idea it was coming?" I ask, thinking back to all the warnings Jack MacDonald gave me.

"Not a clue," Carter explains. "It was basically pack your bags and hit the highway. We were devastated."

"Wow," I say. "What did you do?"

"Well, at first we didn't know what to do. So my wife and I started reading some books and going through a lot of the exercises I put you through. We began thinking about all the things we wanted in life. And then we made a list of all of the things we wanted to avoid."

"That sounds familiar."

"Eventually, we gained the wisdom and confidence to see this as an opportunity to advance ourselves. And I discovered my mission in life."

"But what did you do in the meantime? I mean, how did you keep your bills paid?"

"I took an interim job in a factory. I needed something quick, and I wanted to buy myself some time. Like you, I didn't really like what I was doing before. It was good money, and I learned a lot. But it wasn't what I wanted to spend the rest of my life doing. I had no real passion for it."

"So you used the time working in the factory to think?"

"That's right. I had to plan my escape."

I laugh. "That's an interesting way to put it."

"Well, one thing was for certain. I didn't want to continue working in a factory. And I didn't want to go back into the same field I was in. So I took the time to think about my real purpose in life. I wanted to reinvent myself."

"And this is what you came up with?" I ask.

"That's right. This is my passion in life."

"And you wrote yourself a mission statement?"

Carter laughs. "You bet I did. And if I'm any good at what I'm doing, you should probably be able to guess what it is."

I stop and think for a moment about what Carter has done for me. What has he really given me? I know! "I'll bet your mission is to help people achieve their dreams."

"That about sums it up," he admits.

"Wow! How did you come up with that?"

"I don't know. It just came to me. I started thinking about all the people who could benefit from this type of help. I observed my peers in the factory. I thought about my own father who was miserable throughout most of his career."

"I can relate to that. We sure had a lot of unhappy people working at TYPCO. It was like they had no hope, no vision, no glory."

"Well, that's when I stumbled upon this outplacement firm. A friend of mine told me about it and suggested I check it out. So I did. Three months later, I was working part-time delivering workshops for factory workers who had been outplaced. Three months after that, I quit my factory job and went into it full time. I've been working my way up ever since."

"But how did you choose this vehicle? There must be dozens of ways to help people achieve their dreams."

"I'm sure there are. But this vehicle made sense to me because I was never happy in my original career and neither were many of my friends. Some of us were influenced by our parents who wanted us to become something they had preplanned for us. Others never set any goals at all. But in both cases, people were throwing their lives away. They were wasting their time."

"Like me at TYPCO."

"You and thousands of other people across the country."

"I should have you talk to my oldest son in New York. From what he tells me, he's ready to reinvent himself."

"Why do you say that?"

"Because his dreams are starting to take him in another direction. He's feeling plateaued."

Carter leans forward. "What are his dreams telling him?"

"They're suggesting he leave New York, start a family, maybe go into business for himself."

"What kind of business?"

"I don't know. We haven't really talked any details yet. Remember, this is the same son I haven't talked to in two years."

"I remember you telling me that." Carter pauses. "Well, as his father, what would you say are his moments of bliss?"

"Catching fish," I blurt out without hesitation. "And catching people's attention with creative marketing campaigns."

"What else does he value in life?" Carter asks.

I think for a moment. "Family," I reply. "I think he really values family."

"So why not invite him to join your business?"

"I've thought about that," I say. "But I don't know. I'd hate to ask him to join me and then have the whole thing flop. We're on thin enough ice as it is."

Carter leans back in his chair and smiles. "Have you ever tried doing a flip off a diving board, Wayne?"

I shrug my shoulders. "I don't know. Maybe a long time ago."

"Well, what do you think happens if you don't give it your all?"

"I suppose you land flat on your back."

"That's right. And it hurts. My son made that very clear to me the other day. He got half-way over and then he gave up. He knew what he had to do, and he knew it could be done. But he didn't give it his total commitment. My point is this - what you're setting out to do can be done. But you've got to give it your *total commitment*. Otherwise, you're going to get hurt."

"I realize that. But what about compensation? There's no way I can compete with what Tom's making in New York."

"You're doing it again, Wayne. You're holding yourself back."

"So what are you suggesting? That I ask my son to join me for nothing? Let's be realistic."

Carter sighs. "Why not bring him in as a partner. Offer him a share of the business. Put him in charge of Marketing and Sales. The challenge alone may excite him."

"Alright. You've got my attention."

"But think about this carefully," Carter cautions. "Don't just throw out an invitation without any planning. Show him what his investment and involvement in the business can lead to. Share your vision with him, and let him determine for himself if he shares a common vision. It will be a common vision and a common set of values that will keep your partnership healthy and strong."

"In other words, if we see the same picture in the future and we share the same core values, we can work out all the rest?"

"That's right. It's no different than finding a suitable marriage partner. Common vision and shared values will serve as the most powerful bonding agent."

As Carter says this, I immediately start thinking of Annette. Even though we don't talk about it often, we do share a common vision. We see ourselves in the future doing certain things together and going to certain places together. Whenever I look ahead at all the things I still want to do in my life, Annette is always there."

"Maybe you're right, Carter. Maybe common vision is the missing link in a lot of marriages."

"It isn't just marriages I'm talking about. Common vision applies to any group of people who want to perform well as a team - especially business partnerships. You and Annette and Tom will need to discuss exactly where you see this business going in the future. You'll need to discuss your business philosophy and guiding principles. You'll need to define your mission and your priorities. You'll need to set goals and develop strategies for achieving those goals. Running a successful business builds on the same principles we use as individuals to achieve peak performance. It requires focus and total commitment."

"Now that you mention it, this is the same thing we were starting to do at TYPCO when I left."

"I know that. And that's exactly why I'm telling you this. If you're going to run a successful business, Wayne, you're going to have to learn to become a great team player. Many people fail to understand this. They go into business to be their own boss, or to escape the hassles of the corporate world. These are dangerous assumptions. You will always have a boss - in any business. It will be your customer. And you will always have hassles to deal with and problems to solve. But if you understand the principles of teamwork, and you know how to utilize the resources around you, you will come out on top. All it takes is a clear picture of where you want to go and a total commitment to taking the steps that lead you there. You've got the power within you, Wayne. All you need to do is plug yourself in."

# CHAPTER 27

Annette strolls into the workshop and stands next to my new make-shift desk - an old door laying over two short filing cabinets. I haven't been putting much time into dressing up the workshop. My focus has been on more important things.

"Next week's going to be busy," she says. "I just mailed out twenty-six letters and brochures to local retailers. Now, we've got to follow up with phone calls."

"That's fine. I plan to call each one of them next week. If I get meetings with half of them, we're going to be doing alright."

"And I sent thank you letters to everyone you met with this week."

"Thanks, Nette. I'm sure they'll appreciate that."

Annette is not only efficient, but she is extremely professional. "Do you have anything that has to go out tomorrow?"

"No, I don't think so. Right now, I'm just trying to finish up this proposal for Tom."

"Oh good," Annette says, leaning over to look at it. "Are you going with the option we discussed this morning?"

"That's the one. I'm inviting him to work with us part-time from New York on a straight commission basis. He'll get 15% of anything he can bring in. I'm also offering him an opportunity to invest in the business, and I'm planning to match anything he puts in."

"Are you sure you're ready for this?"

"It's now or never. I don't want to get half-way into this and then fall flat on my back. We've got enough equity in the house to secure a fairly substantial loan. If Tom's willing to take the risk, so am I."

"Good for you," Annette says "I'm glad you want to do this."

"Well, it's like you said before, Nette. This gives Tom a lot of room for testing the water. I don't want to put any pressure on him. If he's interested, he can ease his way in. If he's not, he doesn't have to do anything. At least, we're presenting him with a legitimate option."

"It is exciting to think about, though, isn't it? It's just like that future biography you wrote about yourself. Remember?"

"I remember perfectly. That was Carter's whole point in giving me the exercise. He says that people have to paint a picture of what they want in the future before they can ever hope to become it. This gives people focus and direction. Ultimately, it evokes passion. The mind works primarily with images and pictures. Therefore, vision has a very powerful influence on performance. *People become what they see.*"

"What do you suppose happens when people don't create pictures of what they want in the future?"

I smile, just as Carter did when I asked him the question. "They continue to get the same thing they see in the present. In other words, they reinforce what they already are. If they only see what they are now or what they've been in the past, they continue to get the same results. But if they see something different, like I have learned to do, they can become whatever they see. It's a choice we all have the capacity to make."

Annette continues to listen attentively. Judging by the look on her face, she is relating this to some of her own personal experiences.

"Take me, for instance. I used to see myself as a fat, ugly, tough manager. I hid behind my authority at TYPCO. It didn't matter if people liked me or not. I didn't even like myself. But I had power. And I thought I had control. People had to accept me as I was because I saw no reason to change. And then I learned the truth. I had no real power - at least not in the true sense of the word. And I had no real control. It was all an illusion. I was not the man I had the potential to be. I was cheating myself. And I was cheating the people around me." I hesitate for a moment, shaking my head. "And then I met Carter Johnston. And if he hadn't been so persistent, I would have gone right on cheating myself of the honor and the glory that comes with pursuing your life's dreams. That's when I realized I had to change my focus. I had to see myself as a true winner if I was ever going to become a true winner. No job title or level of income or external incentive could ever match the strength and power that comes with this kind of internal focus."

"That sounds like something I remember Walter saying to you years ago," Annette interjects.

"Yeah, except I wasn't listening. I was so fixed on getting Walter into a job that society deemed successful, that I didn't hear what he was saying. I didn't understand his passion for serving as a change agent for young students and athletes. I didn't feel what he felt going to work each morning. I was simply passing along some of the same conventional information my father passed on to me. I was trying to convince my son to work harder rather than smarter. How ridiculous!"

Annette smiles. "Well, if nothing else, we've all grown wiser through this."

"I'll second that. It's amazing to me how biased a person's perspective can be about certain things. Take Daniel Post, for example. When we were growing up, people always assumed he was such a loser. Yet, look at what he had. He had dreams, and he had passion for those dreams. He had vision, and he had the inner strength and conviction to pursue his vision. He never let the external forces get to him. He never got caught up in the quick fix mentality. He just did it.

"Well, isn't that what Carter has been saying to you all along?" Annette asks. "In the end, you just have to do it."

"That's right. You've got to put your heart into it. You've got to give it your total commitment. Ultimately, that's the only real risk that matters."

The business phone suddenly starts ringing. Annette looks at me and smiles. "Would you like me to get that for you, Dear?"

"That's okay," I say, grabbing the phone. "Woodpecker's. Yes. Yes. No problem, Daniel. Yes. You'll have them Friday morning. Thank you."

"Who was that?" she asks after I hang up the phone.

I stand up and face her. Her eyes scan my face looking for a clue. "It's time to open the champagne," I laugh. "That was Daniel Post. He just ordered 75 feeders. He says his customers love them and he wants to send out samples to some of the other franchises."

Annette wraps her arms around me and whispers in my ear. "We're on our way, Wayne!"

# CHAPTER 28

"Walt, it's Dad," I say into the phone.

"Hey, Dad! How goes the pecking?" he laughs. Walter always seems to be in a such a good mood.

"Well, the pecking's coming along. We just got our first order and we have a lot of samples out in circulation. It shouldn't be too long before people start taking an interest."

"No doubt about that," the young man says. "By the way, some of the kids in my class want to know if they can start selling your products door-to-door to raise money for the school. They really think they're great."

I laugh. "Gee, I don't know. I'll have to look into that."

"You should, Dad. It might be another angle for you. So anyway, what's on you mind?"

I take a deep breath. I'm not sure how Walter is going to perceive the news about my inviting Tom into the business. I decide to pose it in the form of a question. "How would you feel if Tom were to join Woodpecker's?"

Walter starts laughing. "Are you kidding?! That would be great!"

"Well, it's not news yet. I just wanted to know how you would feel. Your mom and I are planning to ask Tom if he would consider joining us - at least part-time for awhile, and we wanted to talk to you about it first."

"Dad, that's fantastic. Wow! Talk about doing a one-eighty!"

"We're also planning to offer him an opportunity to invest in the business. You know, buy some stock, come in as an equity partner."

"Does that mean you're selling stock?" Walter's question comes as a surprise. "Can I buy some?"

"You want to buy some stock?" I ask.

"Sure, how much are you selling it for?"

"Well, right now, it's a buck a share."

"Good. I'll take 1000 shares. Is that okay?"

I start laughing. That's probably Walter's entire savings account, yet he acts as if it's petty cash. "You've got a deal, Son."

"Now, I realize that isn't going to weigh much compared to what Tom might invest, but I want to do what I can."

"Walt, you don't have to invest in the business."

"I appreciate that, Dad. But I want to invest in the business. The way I see it, you guys are going to do wonders with the place and I want in on the action. Let's just say this is part of my retirement account."

How ironic. Now I have money coming into the business and I'm not even asking for it.

"And what about your future, Walt? Would you ever consider joining the business?"

Walter hesitates for a moment. I'm afraid he senses I'm putting pressure on him. "I appreciate the thought, Dad. But I'm really happy doing what I'm doing right now. *You know, reinventing yourself doesn't always mean changing jobs. I try to reinvent myself everyday by simply expanding my knowledge base and doing a better job at what I'm already doing.*"

"I understand, Walt. Believe me, I understand."

"That doesn't mean I don't want to serve as a resource to your business. I just don't want to give up what I'm already doing."

"I respect that, Son. And I don't want you to feel like you're under any pressure. I just want you to know that the door is always open. You have already helped me in more ways than you can imagine."

"Thanks, Dad. I'm really proud of you."

As Walter says this, I begin wondering how long it's been since my sons could say this about me. How long has it been since Tom and Walter could look at me and honestly say "That's my Dad. He's a great guy!"

"Say, by the way, Walt. I haven't forgotten about those audio tapes you loaned me. Can I give them back the next time I see you?"

"No problem. Just promise me that you'll listen to them again in the meantime."

"What do you mean?" I ask.

"You'll absorb more the second time through," he says. "Trust me. It's time well spent."

I trust his advice. "Alright, I'll do it."

"What did you think about the one on improvisation, anyway?"

"I liked it. But I found it a little contradictory at times. I mean, here I am getting all this advice about planning grilled into me and along comes this author suggesting I learn to use improvisation as a strategy."

Walter laughs. "He's right, though, Dad. It's just like in football. Surely, you have to have a gameplan. But you can't predict everything that is going to happen. Life is full of uncertainty. You have to learn to adapt quickly and rethink your strategy to overcome unexpected circumstances."

"I suppose you're right. Chances are, I'm going to have to do a lot of improvisation to get my business off the ground. I'm already running into obstacles I didn't anticipate."

"That's where most people fall flat on their face. They don't adapt quickly enough to keep them moving in the direction they want to go. They either get knocked in another direction or they give up. It's like all those New Year's resolutions that people set and then blow off two weeks later."

As Walter says this, I think about all the improvisation he's had to do to achieve his purpose in life. When he had football taken away from him, he improvised. He found teaching and coaching. I suppose if he had that taken away from him, he would find something else to keep him moving in a productive and fulfilling direction. Clearly, Walter would never give up. And neither would Annette or Carter or Daniel Post or anyone else who is determined to lead a rich and meaningful life.

"Do you ever think about things you'd do differently in life?" I ask.

"In the past or in the future?" he asks.

"Both, I suppose."

"Never in the past. Always in the future."

"What do you mean by that?" I inquire.

"What's past is past. And what's present is present. The only thing a person can change is the future. Why worry about the rest? It is as it is."

"I guess you're right."

"Don't get me wrong," Walter continues. "I think about the past and the present a lot - but only to evaluate my outcomes and experiences. There is a lot to be gained by assessing past results. If nothing else, you can learn what *not* to do to avoid getting results you *don't* want."

Isn't that the truth? If you want to reinvent yourself, you've got to begin by taking a close look at yourself. If you aren't the person you want to be, you've got to define the person you want to become. And if you aren't doing the things which matter most in your life, you've got to stop and ask yourself why. Every one of us has the power to change at anytime. And contrary to popular belief, it doesn't have to take a lifetime. It may take a lifetime of passionate commitment to maintain a change, but the change itself starts the moment we decide to move in another direction. *This is the moment of truth. This is what personal leadership is all about.*

# PART VII

# Count Your Blessings

"According to the depths from which you draw your life,
such is the depth of your accomplishment."

*Emerson*

# EPILOGUE

As I pull out of my driveway, I begin reflecting on the past twelve months of my life. That's when I was informed I would no longer be working for TYPCO. At first, I felt cheated and humiliated. During the following two months, I allowed these feelings to sabotage my life. I saw myself as a victim and I used this as an excuse to complain about, rather than challenge, the outcome. I also viewed my one-time friend and former boss, Jack MacDonald, as the reason for my problems. I was not at fault. He was. He betrayed me. He destroyed my life.

Then I met Carter Johnston. And with Carter's help, I reinvented myself. I am now a free man, pursuing my dreams and enjoying my life as it was meant to be enjoyed. My oldest son has since joined me in the business, and we are achieving great success. He came aboard full-time two months ago, right after landing a big pilot deal with a national nursery and garden center. Thanks to Tom, we have now been written up in several publications and we're starting to do some promotional work with a local school system.

We're currently manufacturing about 1500 products a month, well below capacity, but we're learning fast. I expect we'll be up to 3000 products a month within another six months. Our goal for year three is to then double that amount to 6000 products per month, and our goal for year four is to double it once more to 12,000 units per month. Eventually, I'm going to have to bring on additional help to meet demand.

Tom is very excited about the business. His investment of $10,000, plus my match, has given us plenty of working capital to build some inventory. This enables us to meet the just-in-time delivery requirements of some of our larger target accounts - which Tom is handling - and it gives me a chance to iron out some of the kinks in our manufacturing system. Eventually, we'll move to more of a "pull" system whereby we manufacture directly to order, reducing our inventory costs.

Tom is also seeing a lot of his friend Kelsey in nearby Rhode Island and our relationship as father and son is growing stronger each day. I now realize that my relationships with others are a reflection of the relationship I have with myself.

Annette is on top of the world. She still works full-time at the law firm, but she is anxiously awaiting the day when she can join us full time. Right now, her income is still helping us stay afloat.

Tom is still working off commission and I'm not getting paid anything yet. Everything we make goes back into the business. Once we hit 3000 units a month, we can both start collecting a more stable paycheck.

We're also exploring a new line of products - ready-to-assemble doghouses. Kelsey came up with the idea after visiting our shop. Who knows? We may even have a catalogue of our own someday.

As I drive East across town, I think about where I might be right now if none of this had happened. Would I be happy? Would I have passion for my work? Would I have my family back together? Would I have made new friends in Carter Johnston and Daniel Post? Would I have lost 27 pounds? Would I have gained the invaluable insight I have gained? I hardly think so. The truth is, I have been blessed. I have been given a chance to start over again.

And as much as I'd like to give myself credit for turning this negative situation into a positive one, I didn't really do it alone. I've had help all along the way. But there is still one man who doesn't realize how much he's done for me.

I turn into an old and familiar driveway. There at the end of it is Jack MacDonald and his son Kevin playing basketball. As I approach, they both stop and look up. Suddenly, Jack tosses the ball to Kevin and starts walking slowly towards my car. I stop the car and climb out.

Jack reaches his hand out. "Wayne, you look fantastic!"

"Thanks, Jack," I say, holding back a smile. "I owe it all to you."

"Hardly," he chuckles. "What did I do? Starve you?"

"On the contrary," I reply. "You nourished me. You put me on the greatest diet any man could ever experience."

Jack shakes his head. "I don't believe it. I would have hardly recognized you. Wow! What a surprise!"

I laugh. "I just wanted to come by to give you something and say thanks. I never realized how much I was limiting myself until I was put to the test. I'm a new man, now. I've competely reinvented myself."

"Well, you can't just show up here and not stay for awhile. C'mon inside and say hello to Judy. She'd love to see you."

"Hold on a minute." I reach into the back seat and grab a box. "Here's something for you and Kevin to work on together," I say, handing the nicely packaged, ready-to-assemble birdfeeder to Jack. "Hopefully, it will give you guys some quality time together."

"Thanks, Wayne. This looks like fun!"

"It's my favorite model," I reply. "I was going to assemble it for you but then I didn't want to take away from the father-son experience."

Jack hesitates for a moment and examines the box more

carefully. "You mean to tell me you created this product?" he then asks in disbelief.

"That's right," I laugh. "I am the Woodpecker."

Jack appears stunned. "Wayne, this is incredible! This is fantastic!"

"Like I said, I've reinvented myself."

"Well, c'mon. You've got to come inside and say hello to Judy. She's going to love this."

"I'll stay for a few minutes," I say. "But I really can't stay too long."

"Hi, Mr. Peterson!" Kevin yells from the basketball court. "Nice to see you again."

"Likewise, Kevin. How's the game?"

"Getting better!" the young man returns. "I think we're going to be pretty good this year. Of course, we can't do much worse than we did last year," he laughs.

"I know how you feel," I shout. "Just remember, most problems are really opportunities in disguise. Take advantage of this!"

"That's an interesting observation, Wayne," Jack whispers. "Care to elaborate?"

"Let's just say I've had a lot of time to reevaluate my life," I offer. "And, until now, I never had a strategy to realize my true potential. Matter of fact, I never had any plan at all."

Jack reflects on what I say. "That sounds a lot like what we've been going through over at TYPCO. We're discovering new opportunities every day."

As we enter the house, I see Judy in the kitchen. She looks up. "Wayne Peterson? Is that you?"

"It's me, Judy, in the flesh."

She runs over and gives me a big hug. "I've been worried about you."

"Well, what can I say? I needed some time to think things through."

Judy steps back and studies me. "By the looks of it, you've been doing a lot more than thinking. You look terrific!"

Jack speaks next. "Wayne was about to share his formula for success. Just take a look at what he's doing now." Jack hands Judy the birdfeeder I gave him.

"Wow! You made this, Wayne?"

"He not only made it," Jack continues. "He owns the company. Why don't you join us out back on the deck to hear how he did it?"

"I wouldn't miss it for the world," Judy says. "Can I bring you guys a cup of coffee?"

"Just water for me," I reply.

"Actually, water sounds good," Jack follows.

Judy nods and then disappears. Minutes later, she joins us on the deck. "So what secrets have I missed?"

"Nothing yet, Dear," Jack responds. "Wayne was just catching up on some TYPCO news."

"It sure sounds like TYPCO is a heck of a lot better off without me," I laugh. Jack and Judy look awkwardly at each other. "Well, c'mon, admit it," I continue. "I was in the way. I was a bottleneck. It's obvious."

"Well, it hasn't exactly been the same around there without you, Wayne," Jack admits tactfully.

"I'll bet," I interject playfully. "You were right, you know."

"About what?" Jack asks.

"About getting me out of there."

"For TYPCO?" he asks.

"Not just TYPCO," I explain. "You did the right thing for me, too."

Judy sits quietly as Jack and I dance our way through this

awkward conversation. I sense from her expression that she and Jack have lost many nights' sleep over this.

"I did?" Jack says.

"That's right. I just didn't see it right away. You set me free. And you were decent enough to give me the help of a remarkable man, Carter Johnston."

Jack sits silently.

I continue. "Between your making the tough call and Carter persevering through the blockades I put up, you two changed my life."

Jack holds his hand up. "No. I have to disagree with you there. You are the only one who can change your life. You have to make the decision."

Judy smiles. "That's true, Wayne. The choice is up to the individual."

"Alright, then, you gave me the push I needed to get started and I took charge from there. How's that?"

Jack nods his head slightly.

"Well, you did the right thing, and I just want you both to know how much I appreciate it."

"You're welcome," Jack says with disbelief.

"So tell us more about Woodpecker's," Judy prompts.

Twenty minutes later, I have given my two old friends a complete summary of my tumultuous year. Both appear to be intrigued by my new passion in life, my renewed relationship with my oldest son, and the amazing insights I have gained during the past twelve months.

I conclude. "If nothing else, I've learned that the true meaning of success is the on-going expansion of myself and the realization of my goals. It is waking up everyday appreciating the opportunities I have and finding the courage to seize them. Success is a journey, not a destination, and I still have a long way to go."

"Your Carter Johnston sounds a lot like Jordan McKay," Jack says, referring to the consultant who facilitated the TYPCO revolution.

"Yeah, I thought the same thing. Isn't it amazing how one person can influence the lives of so many others?"

"It sure is," Jack responds. "That's what's got me thinking about making a change."

Judy and I both look at Jack in astonishment.

"What is that supposed to mean?" Judy asks cautiously.

"It's just an idea I've been playing around with lately," Jack explains. "I'm starting to feel like I need to make a change. I can't help but feel like I have a higher purpose in life than the one I'm serving at TYPCO."

Judy looks at her husband. "You've never said anything about this before."

"I know," Jack continues. "It's just a feeling I've been having lately."

I smile to myself. Somehow, I can sense what's just around the corner for Jack MacDonald. How ironic!

"So you're thinking about leaving TYPCO?" Judy pursues.

"Not right away," Jack explains. "But I am starting to think about a new career." Jack hesitates and looks from Judy to me. "I'm thinking about going into consulting. You know, like Jordan McKay is doing. I think it would be fascinating."

"Have you discussed this with Jordan?" Judy asks.

"No. Not yet."

"Why would you want to make a change now?" I ask.

Jack pauses for a moment. "Because I want to go *beyond* what I'm doing now. It's like you said before. Success is about on-going expansion. I want to go beyond TYPCO. I want to help other people in management achieve what I have achieved at TYPCO. I want to give something back."

"It's better than becoming plateaued," I interject.

"I trust you're right about that, Wayne. And, after hearing you tell your story, I'm encouraged to move ahead. It's time to turn my dream into reality. Believe it or not, Wayne Peterson, you are an inspiration."

I turn and smile at my renewed friend. Adversity holds a greater advantage.

# WAYNE'S SEVEN LAWS OF SUCCESS

1.  KNOW YOUR PURPOSE: Imagine you have all the time and money in the world. What would you be doing? How would you be spending your time? Define your special gifts and unique talents. Think about your past accomplishments and identify the skills you used to achieve these goals. What are your core competencies? What are your moments of biss? What is your core purpose in life? Take fullest advantage of your greater gifts - for maximum personal benefit and for the benefit of others. Follow your purpose, not your paycheck.

2.  DEFINE YOUR CHARACTER: Know who you are and envision your ideal self in the future. Find positive role models and mentors to emulate. Study them and learn from them. Surround yourself with winning attitudes. Write your ideal biography ten years from now. Prepare your own inspiring eulogy. Describe how you want to be remembered. Define the legacy you wish to leave behind. Create a list of guiding principles and use these "constants" to generate honor, self-respect and integrity.

3.  UNDERSTAND YOUR COMPETITION: Carefully examine the forces against you - both internal and external. What are your core beliefs? How do you perceive yourself? What is holding you back? What will cause you to fail? What are your constraints? What obstacles must you overcome to achieve your vision of success?

4. CHALLENGE YOUR ASSUMPTIONS. Stretch yourself. Keep an open mind. Tap into the abundant resources that surround you. Pay attention to the information and services available. Observe the people around you. Network. Read everything you can. Commit to lifelong learning. Change your beliefs and you change your outcomes. You may be your own worst enemy.

5. CONFRONT YOUR FEARS: Step up to the plate. Put yourself to the test. Trust your instincts. Learn to live with uncertainty. Do not fear mistakes. Look beyond your fears to a compelling picture of yourself in the future. Accept the fact that in order to succeed you must learn to overcome adversity. Take responsibility for your own actions and outcomes. Make a decision. Commit yourself.

6. PLUG YOURSELF IN: Take charge of your life. Recognize that job planning and career planning are part of life planning. Set your priorities and seek balance and congruence between work, family, play and self. Develop and execute your plan for success. Manage your time around your priorities. Look for ways to turn work into play. Start now to build the life you most desire.

7. COUNT YOUR BLESSINGS: Have faith. Recognize that you are not alone. Get in touch with nature. Respect yourself. Appreciate who you are. Reconcile with your enemies. Build bridges, not barriers. Free your soul. Find the silver-linings. Make the most out of what you have. Take time to laugh. Enjoy life. *Happiness is a choice!*

# ABOUT THE AUTHOR

John Murphy is president of Venture Management Consultants, Inc., a firm specializing in creating high performance work environments. As a practitioner of these principles, John advises people worldwide on how to achieve peak performance results.

John is a graduate of the University of Notre Dame and the University of Michigan Graduate Business School's Human Resource Executive Program. John has also written *"Pulling Together: The Power of Teamwork"* and *"Agent of Change: Leading a Cultural Revolution."*

John resides in Grand Rapids, Michigan with his wife, Stephanie, and four children.

# Other Books
## by John Murphy

*Pulling Together:*
*The Power of Teamwork*

*Agent of Change:*
*Leading A Cultural Revolution*

For more information or to order books,

Please Call,
(616) 942-2525

Visa and MasterCard Accepted